Global Health Narratives

GLOBAL HEALTH NARRATIVES

A Reader for Youth

Edited, and with an Introduction by
Emily Mendenhall

Foreword by **Kate Winskell**

Illustrations by **Hannah Adams**

University of New Mexico Press

Albuquerque

© 2009 by the University of New Mexico Press
All rights reserved. Published 2009
Printed in the United States of America

15 14 13 12 11 10 09   1 2 3 4 5 6 7

Library of Congress Cataloging-in-Publication Data

Global health narratives : a reader for youth / compiled, edited,
and with an introduction by Emily Mendenhall ; foreword
by Kate Winskell ; illustrations by Hannah Adams.
            p. cm.
Includes index.
ISBN 978-0-8263-4605-6 (pbk. : alk. paper)
1. World health—Juvenile literature. 2. Readers—Health.
I. Mendenhall, Emily, 1982–
        RA441
        362.1—dc22

                        2008043123

Designed and typeset by Mina Yamashita.
Composed in Minion Pro, an Adobe Original typeface
designed by Robert Slimbach. Display composed in
Frutiger 77 Black Condensed, designed by Adrian Frutiger.
Printed by Thomson-Shore, Inc. on 55# Natures Natural.

For Barbara Bowers Mendenhall

Education either functions as an instrument which is used to facilitate integration of the younger generation into the logic of the present system and bring about conformity or it becomes the practice of freedom, the means by which men and women deal critically and creatively with reality and discover how to participate in the transformation of their world.

—Paolo Freire, Brazilian educator

In the global era, global health equity, more than ever before, must be a goal of any serious ethical character.

—Dr. Paul Farmer, U.S. anthropologist and physician

Contents

Part 5: Africa

Part 6: Europe

Foreword

Kate Winskell

Reflecting on the power of art and literature in his Nobel Prize acceptance speech, the Russian writer Alexander Solzhenitsyn described their capacity to recreate "in the flesh an unknown experience" and allow us "to possess it as our own." They are, he said, "the only substitute for an experience we have never lived through."

The beautiful narratives in this book bridge cultural divides, allowing readers to experience vicariously the lived reality of key global health issues from the perspective of children and young people around the world. We empathize with the inspiring young characters introduced to us in these stories as they face challenges to their own health and that of their loved ones and communities.

In the words of cultural psychologist Jerome Bruner, stories have the remarkable capacity to allow us to "perfink"—perceive, think, and feel all at once. One of the things that makes them so powerful is that they permit us to alternate between being absorbed in the story and reflecting on its implications. By drawing us in emotionally while at the same time leaving room for critical analysis, narratives can help us feel our way into new ways of thinking. When used as a teaching resource, stories can be a particularly powerful tool for triggering collective critical thinking about the root causes of social injustice.

In this book, public health practitioners and activists share stories, drawing on their own experiences around the globe. This project began to take shape during an interdisciplinary seminar on narrative and health convened by Emory University's Center for Health, Culture, and Society (CHCS). We at CHCS were happy to provide Emily Mendenhall with financial support as she used her inimitable energies to develop the concept and rally her collaborators. Through their creative energies, the authors bring global health to life in a compelling way. These culturally sensitive stories will allow young readers to empathize with other young people around the world and will provide them with inspiring examples of compassion, courage, and social engagement. The stories will also encourage readers to reflect on the global inequities that fuel ill health. We hope they will provide a trigger for personal and social transformation.

Acknowledgments

During a guest lecture he gave to Dr. Stanley Foster's international health policy class at the Rollins School of Public Health, Dr. William Foege welcomed students to the workforce of builders for a better tomorrow. He observed that building the field of public health will, like the pyramids, take lifetimes, and, as with the pyramids, the result will be an improved environment, a better world. Thank you, Dr. Stanley Foster, for exposing your students to many incredible leaders in public health and encouraging us not only to reduce disease but also to fight poverty and inequality.

Putting this book together was possible only through a great collaboration of dedicated public health scholars, clinicians, activists, teachers, and writers. Thank you to the incredible authors highlighted in it. Your wisdom, passion, and time invested in this work seep from its pages. A special thank you is warranted to three dedicated teachers, Jenny Rawlings Wernly, Alison Holby, and Jackie Protos. The collaboration of alumni from Davidson College provided much needed support in many stages of this project. Also, thank you to additional contributors of ideas and moral support, including Dr. Sarah Willen, Dr. Elizabeth Corrie, Dr. Ryan A. Brown, Ajay Pillarisetti, Adam D. Koon, Jennifer Kuzara, Gurkiran Sardar, Dr. Mba Atinga, Sharon Adelle Greene, and MJ Devaney. A special thank you to Lisa Pacheco, our editor at University of New Mexico Press, for believing in our book and providing support throughout.

Thank you to the Hubert Department of Global Health for guiding and inspiring many students, alumni, and public health projects around the world. Thank you to Dr. Peter Brown and Dr. Kate Winskell for your initial support of this book, which ignited the process of planning and writing, as well as for helping to secure the intellectual and fiscal support of the Center for Health, Culture, and Society at Emory University.

Finally, a spicy thank you to my extraordinary family and dear friends for your continual moral support and for your multiple conversations about this idea and many readings of the stories, all of which has significantly contributed to the pages that follow.

Introduction

Emily Mendenhall

Dr. John Snow thought something was fishy. Others proclaimed that the cholera epidemic was caused by something in the air, but John knew it was something more. He went from house to house, questioning his neighbors about where they worked and what they ate, seeking what they had in common. After much investigation, he was led to the Broad Street pump. In 1854, John was one of the first doctors to associate disease with the environment, an association he was able to make because he had discovered that the polluted well caused the cholera epidemic in London. The field of public health grew from John's discovery. Today, public health aims to solve health problems by examining the many contributors to disease.

Public health is important because prevention is key to preserving a person's health. Significant public health efforts include providing vaccinations, supplying education, and encouraging healthy behaviors. Making healthy choices, such as getting vaccinated for childhood diseases, prevents ailments for the individual and improves health at the population level. As biomedicine continues to turn to "band-aids" and "treatments" for ailments *after* they occur, public health works to educate people about prevention *before* the onset of disease or disability.

The essential reason for this text is to provide youth with a context for understanding the importance of healthy communities. Public health takes many forms and includes such projects as 1) vaccinating children to prevent polio and measles; 2) reducing maternal mortality; 3) encouraging people to eat diverse and healthy foods; 4) providing essential medicines for individuals suffering from malaria, tuberculosis, and HIV/AIDS; 5) unveiling the silence of depression;

6) improving water sources for communities who subsist on unsafe water; 7) reducing stigma for people living with diseases such as obesity or AIDS; 8) preventing chronic diseases such as diabetes and hypertension; 9) smoking cessation; and 10) increasing people's access to health care. This list is in no way exhaustive of the many forms public health programs take within communities or even of how public health is presented in this book.

The definition of health used in this book includes physiological, psychological, and social aspects. "Health," as the preamble to the 1946 constitution of the World Health Organization puts it, "is a state of complete physical, mental, and social well-being and not merely the absence of disease or infirmity." It is important to remember that an individual's sickness is not always visible and that depression is one of the most pervasive epidemics worldwide. The cause of health problems can also be difficult to trace if they are linked to environmental problems. Dangerous pathogens and viruses are often easier to diagnose than high levels of mercury in one's water, for example. Although physical, emotional, and behavioral disorders are all defined at the individual level, environmental factors affect health at the community level, which means many people can be affected by one polluted source. Because such a wide variety of factors affect health, the best way to improve public health is to address these broader factors in combination with biological- and individual-centered approaches to health.

The narratives developed for this book demonstrate that global health is not only about reducing disease burden but also about monitoring the environment (such as homes, workplaces, schools, urban parks, and farmlands) to improve overall community health. Global health disparities often result from structural violence, which means that social structures outside of individuals' control (such as poverty and unemployment) prevent them from meeting basic needs (such as eating healthy foods and finding sustainable housing). This means that disease may not result from the choices one makes; rather, disease may result from physical and emotional distress caused by political-economic problems such as poverty and poor working conditions. For example, if a family lives near a river, and waste from a factory contaminates the water upstream, then the family's water supply may be unsafe. The family's sickness results from the inability to find a cleaner water source and the factory's noncompliance with governmental regulations of waste disposal. Another example is HIV and AIDS. Many people affected by HIV and AIDS are children; some children are born with the disease and must live with the virus their whole lives. Many children who are not themselves HIV positive are nonetheless affected by the disease because they lose a parent or sibling. In this case, their suffering is a result of association with the virus, which they do not have the power to prevent.

The importance of global health stems from its systematic approach to solving health problems by identifying the source. In order to develop long-term solutions to public health issues, a global perspective is not only useful but also critical. Furthermore, as the population, even within the United States, continues to become more diverse, it becomes ever more necessary for youth to learn about global health issues. These narratives, rich in detail of different communities and customs, focus on the most critical basic element of any thriving community: health. By providing these narratives, we aim to raise critical public health consciousness in the community—in your classrooms with your teachers, at your lunch tables with your friends, and at your kitchen tables with your family—so that the next generation will be more knowledgeable than the last. To help teachers in assigning stories for their classes to read, each narrative has been given a reading assessment number ranging from one to five based on writing difficulty, narrative length, and maturity level. Teaching guides and additional resources are available online at www.ghn4c.org.

This book is a guide to educate youth about disease, inequality, and the environment.

JAPAN

MONGOLIA

CHINA

INDIA

NEPAL

THAILAND

Part 1

ASIA

1

Toshio and the Crane

Jackie Protos

"Toshio and the Crane" tells the story of a boy living on the outskirts of Hiroshima, Japan, and the devastation of health that followed on nuclear warfare and radiation sickness. The exposure to radiation has caused as many deaths as the initial explosion of the Atomic Bomb. By reading this narrative, students should begin to understand that exposure to radiation and chemicals (often found in herbicides, insecticides, foods, and ground water) can cause cancer. Cancer is the uncontrolled growth of cells that take nutrition and blood supply from the rest of the body.

"I can't do it anymore!" Toshio shrieked and crumpled up his eighth piece of writing paper. When had school become so hard? Why was his teacher so mean? Writing five paragraphs on a famous person in Japan? What was he thinking?

"Toshio, those are not words a wise man utters," spoke Toshio's grandfather from the corner of the room. There Oji-san sat reading. His round face always nuzzled in literature. His smoke-colored hair always uncombed, whisked over his tiny oval glasses. He read everything: all the bits of the newspaper, page after page of books, the backs of cereal boxes, lines on people's faces, everything. Oji-san not only read everything; he *knew* everything. Toshio loved that about his dear grandfather.

Toshio stared at the crumpled pieces of paper. His silence signified his failure. Then, Toshio heard Oji-san rise from his worn leather chair. He heard the slow, steady scuffle of Oji-san's slippers move across the tatami floor. Toshio braced himself for the lecture ahead: Oji-san lowered his eyes, crossed his arms, and gave out a sigh that made it sound like he could make the clouds move. Next, Oji-san did an unusual thing. He sat down right beside Toshio and tousled his hair.

Oji-san took his time picking up each of the eight pieces of crumpled paper. His joints creaked as he slowly unfolded Toshio's failed writing attempts. Oji-san's hands looked as wrinkled as the paper he was unfolding. Oji-san smirked and said, "Toshio, you always have the ability to create something beautiful—there's always more to come."

Oji-san could captivate a roomful of bees buzzing for honey. Toshio, too, was hooked. He watched as Oji-san rubbed away the wrinkles in the paper. Oji-san looked like he was straightening the waves of the sea. He then started folding the paper into a square, then one triangle after another. He sat there with a fixed look on his face, the same look he would get when he was reading an interesting story in the newspaper or a captivating tale in a book. He kept folding the paper, smaller and smaller, until Toshio could only see Oji-san's hands working in swift pace.

"*Subarashii*" exclaimed Oji-san—the Japanese word for "excellent." "There you have it, a famous person for you to write about." Toshio looked at the paper that Oji-san had folded—but all he saw was an origami paper crane. Though he was impressed that his grandfather still remembered how to make the figure, he hardly thought this was worth writing about.

"Oji-san, are you sure? This is but a crane, a silly paper crane, Oji-san" was Toshio's combative reply. Oji-san stared determinedly at the origami crane. He knew he had a lesson to share with his young grandson.

Oji-san went on to tell a tale that Toshio would never forget. Toshio unfolded his arms and rested one hand on Oji-san's knee. He always knew there was more to come with Oji-san.

"Toshio, my dear one. This crane is not the famous person you should write about, Sadako is. Sadako was a very famous girl in Japan. She was your exact age—only twelve—when she became so well known. And I'll tell you why.

"Sadako loved sports just like you do, Toshio. She could play soccer even better than you can. Townspeople said Sadako was so skilled she could kick a soccer ball over the rooftop of her own house! She used to play hour after hour in one of the rice paddies on her parents' farm in Hiroshima, Japan. A small town in southern Japan, Hiroshima was not known for much but peaceful rivers and family-owned factories. Sadako dreamed of representing Hiroshima as a famous athlete on the first Japanese woman's soccer team. But it was not her athletics that made her so famous.

"Instead circumstances beyond Sadako's control gave her fame. One sweet-smelling summer day, Sadako was out in the paddies kicking the soccer ball as usual. Her new white shoes were shining in the streaks of the sun. All of a sudden, Sadako heard a large blast and she felt the ground below shake like a blanket in a storm. She hit the hard soil beneath her. Sadako's small hands rested on the ground, and she felt terrible vibrations moving beneath her. Could this be an earthquake like the ones she'd read about?

"The shaking ceased, and Sadako finally got the courage to move up from the rice paddy. Her eyes peered over the paddy, but all she saw was dark gray smoke. Smoke was everywhere, from the tips of the clouds all the way down to the soil below. The smoke was so thick Sadako could not even see her now-stained shoes on her feet. She coughed and coughed and rubbed her eyes, but the smoke would not go away. Her coughs just bounced around in the silence of that gruesome gray air. Sadako then did all she knew to do: she ran; she ran and ran and sprinted off for home.

"As soon as Sadako reached her home, a sharp siren pierced her ears. No birds could be heard, no leaves whispering in the wind, just that severe sound of the siren blaring through her house. Soon Sadako smelled fire from far away. She tried to block out the noises and the smells, but her efforts were useless. Sadako's head pounded from all the commotion; she clung to her mother's apron, it being the only comfort she could find.

"It was not until a few hours later that Sadako's mother told her what happened. It was a time of war in Japan: World War II. Japan had just been attacked. A smoke bomb had been dropped on downtown Hiroshima because of the war. But Sadako's mother said how lucky their family was because they lived on a farm outside the city; they were safe.

"Sadako knew that the smoke bomb must have been terrible for the people in Hiroshima city. Thousands of people died instantly from the bomb. Sadako cried for her school friends that lost their lives, she cried for fathers that were in the war, and she cried for strangers she did not know."

"But Oji-san, I know better than that. I know a smoke bomb couldn't kill anybody. They must have been mistaken," interrupted Toshio.

"You are right, my smart grandson. They later learned that the smoke bomb was much more powerful than anyone could have imagined. It was not made of smoke; instead it was made of dangerous atomic particles. It was the first atomic bomb ever dropped in the world. Many people died when the bomb dropped from a plane in the sky. But worse was what it did to the health of people for years to come. Day after day, Sadako read newspaper reports of people dying. She did not understand why people were dying even after the bomb was dropped. What was happening?

"People were forced to see the haunting effects of cancer. Cancer, Toshio, is when cells in your body are infected and grow out of control. Radiation waves from the bomb caused cancer in people all over Hiroshima. No one knew how to treat the disease. Still today, people are unsure how to cure cancer. Far more Japanese people died from cancer than from the actual bomb itself. This is what happened to Sadako.

"Sadako developed leukemia, cancer of her white blood cells, caused by radiation from the bomb. Some of Sadako's friends died from the disease. Instead of crying for her friends, Sadako decided to dream for them. She had heard an old tale that if you made a thousand origami cranes, any wish you made would come true. And so she set forth on her mission. She folded paper like the crumpled paper before you, she folded newspaper, she folded pages from books, she even folded bubble gum wrappers. She folded origami cranes every day. Even when she was in pain, she never lost hope. Sadako strung her cranes on yarn in her room. When she grew sicker, she glued the cranes on the walls of her hospital room. Friends started to visit Sadako and help her craft origami cranes. On one special day, a woman showed up at Sadako's hospital door with an entire boxful of paper cranes. She had heard of Sadako's story and driven five hours just to meet her. People from all over wanted to help make Sadako's wish come true. Still, doctors could not cure her cancer. Sadako died later that year."

Toshio bounced up on his bare feet and shouted at his grandfather. "Didn't she make a thousand cranes? Couldn't more people have helped her?"

"Oh, Sadako had plenty of cranes. She had made over thirteen hundred by the time she died. But you see, Toshio, her wish was not for her own life. Sadako's wish was that children in the future would live in a peaceful world.

"In Hiroshima today, there is a memorial for Sadako. Thousands upon thousands of people visit that site and bring a thousand cranes for peace. Sadako's wish renews itself in each of those cranes. Sadako's wish even rests in the crane sitting before you now."

Toshio looked at the crane that Oji-san had fashioned from the crumpled paper. He grabbed his own piece of crumpled paper and instead of folding a crane, he started writing his story about Sadako.

Oji-san left Toshio to do his work. He went back to reading his paper and soon settled into snores for the night. Meanwhile, Toshio kept writing his paper on Sadako. When Oji-san awoke the next morning, he found a fresh origami crane resting on the table beside him.

Next to the crane stood a note that made Oji-san's eyes and heart smile. "More to come" was it all said.

The following day at school, Toshio's classmates turned in their papers, placing them on the teacher's desk. Toshio waited until the last of the papers was added to the stack. He then reached into his pocket and pulled out the crumpled paper crane that Oji-san had made the night before. Toshio placed the crane on top of the papers and went quietly back to his desk.

When Toshio's teacher, Shibata-sensei, collected the papers, he looked inquisitively at the origami crane. In a most grumpy growl, Shibata-sensei asked, "Who turned in this crane instead of a paper? WHO?"

Toshio stared down at his hands and wished for the wisdom of Oji-san. He inched out of his seat and said "Please teacher, do not grow angry. I have a story to tell."

After quickly pulling out his paper, Toshio began reading his paragraphs on Sadako. The class listened to Toshio as he recounted tales of Sadako's life, World War II, the spread of cancer, and the paper cranes. After class, one of Toshio's friends approached him in the hallway. She handed Toshio three freshly made origami cranes with a note that simply read "More to come."

2

The Little *Dhami*

Brandon Kohrt

"The Little Dhami*" describes Naba Raj's life as he struggles with epilepsy in Nepal and relates his experiences seeking medical care from both traditional healers and healers trained in Western medicine. The influence of traditional medicine in people's spiritual and physical lives should be noted, along with the importance of medical technology in curing illnesses that are not easily healed by traditional medicine. This narrative also teaches about epilepsy, an illness affecting children around the world, and highlights how some peoples interpret this illness differently from many Americans.*

Naba Raj walked with his family out of his mud and wood house. His parents had explained that he was going to see a *dhami*. For a boy of ten years old he had already seen too many *dhamis* in his life.

"Why do we have to go see another *dhami*?" Naba Raj asked his grandfather, who walked slowly with the young boy. His other family members climbed more quickly up the hill in front of their house.

"*Dhamis* know more about healing than anyone. When my own grandfather was sick, he always went to the *dhami*. He lived to be eighty years old. He never went to a doctor because in those days there were no hospitals or medical doctors in Nepal," Grandfather replied.

Naba Raj had learned in school that the first doctors and hospitals came to Nepal when his father was a young man. Before that, his country of Nepal, bordered by India to the south and Tibet and China to the north, had many kinds of healers, but no doctors. Healers trained in Hindu medicine from India and Buddhist medicine from Tibet worked in many of the cities, but in small villages everyone relied on *dhamis*.

"*Dhamis* have special ways of finding out why we are sick," Naba Raj's grandfather continued. "They know about all the spirits that move in the villages. They know about your life before you were born. They know about curses and ghosts that other people cannot understand. Wait and see; the *dhami* will help us today."

"But, Grandfather, my sickness is getting better," Naba Raj pleaded. Naba Raj had been sick for a long time, but he was feeling healthy again.

"I know that. Today we must do something very important for your sister."

Naba Raj looked into his grandfather's eyes, surrounded by dark folds of wind-burned skin. Naba Raj's worry about the *dhami* faded away as Grandfather smiled and took Naba Raj's hand. He did want to make his sister happy again. Naba Raj blamed himself for his sister's unhappiness.

The first time Naba Raj had seen a *dhami* was two years ago. While in school, his tongue began to tingle, then went numb, and soon he could not move at all. Then everything was gone. His world went black.

When Naba Raj awoke, all his friends and his teacher were staring down at him. He wanted to ask them what happened, but he was so sleepy. His tongue was still numb, and he could not speak. His father came and carried him home. Naba Raj went to sleep in the afternoon and did not wake up until the following morning.

When Naba Raj put on his school uniform and collected his notebook, his father shocked him by saying, "Son, you should not go to school today."

"But, Father, why?" Naba Raj felt rested, could speak again, and was ready for school.

"You had a sickness yesterday," his father explained. "We need to take you to a *dhami* today. Yesterday, when you fell off your stool, you started shaking and moving around. Then you were so sleepy that you wouldn't talk to anyone afterward."

That night, Naba Raj went with his family to the *dhami*'s house. All night long, family and neighbors sat with the *dhami* while he chanted in a language that Naba Raj could not understand. That night, the *dhami* killed a chicken and placed eggs at different intersections on nearby roads. The community tried everything it could to bring good omens to Naba Raj.

After that, everyone thought that Naba Raj would not have any more attacks and blackouts. However, just one week later, his tongue went numb, and the world went black again. The family went to see another *dhami*, this time in a different village. For many months, his family kept visiting *dhamis*, but Naba Raj continued having these attacks at school and at home.

After many months of visiting *dhamis*, Naba Raj's uncle suggested that the family go see a medical doctor at the hospital. The hospital had been built five years earlier, but the family feared going there. Naba Raj's uncle, however, had become good friends with Dr. Sigdel, a doctor from Kathmandu, Nepal's capital city.

"I told Dr. Sigdel about Naba Raj's problem. The doctor said that Naba Raj has epilepsy," Naba Raj's uncle said to the family. Everyone looked at each other. They were very scared. They had never heard this word before. What did it mean?

The next day, the whole family went with Naba Raj to visit Dr. Sigdel at the hospital. When they explained what was happening with Naba Raj, Dr. Sigdel said, "Yes, this is clearly epilepsy. Epilepsy is a sickness that causes people to sometimes lose control of their body. They may think they are asleep, but their bodies move a great deal, and sometimes they can fall and hurt themselves. These attacks are called 'seizures.' It must be very scary for you."

"What can we do about this Dr. Sigdel?" Naba Raj's father asked.

"I can give you medicine, but Naba Raj will need to take it every day," the doctor replied.

"Every day! Oh my goodness!" the family responded with shock. They had never heard of someone taking medicine every day. Sometimes when someone was sick with stomach illness in the village, he would take medicine for a few days.

"Take this medicine for Naba Raj and give it to him every day, then come back and see me in ten days," the doctor suggested.

During those ten days, Naba Raj still had one seizure. Yet, this was an improvement from the previous month when he had attacks nearly every day.

After visiting Dr. Sigdel again, his family members decided they would continue giving Naba Raj his medicine every day because it was helping with the epilepsy.

After months of taking the medicine every day, both Naba Raj and his family were very happy. Naba Raj was only having attacks, what he now called "seizures," every once in a while. But suddenly the family had a new problem!

Naba Raj's sister had been crying in the field outside of their house all day. Naba Raj tried to comfort her, but she refused to talk to anyone. When Naba Raj asked his father what happened, he also did not reply,

Naba Raj was very confused. Finally, he found his grandfather out in another field taking a break while the oxen who were resting from plowing the rice patty terraces drank water.

"Grandfather, what is wrong with Sister? No one will tell me what is going on."

"It is a very sad situation, Grandson. Did you know that your sister was to be married this spring?" Naba Raj nodded to his grandfather. He knew that his older sister would soon be married to a young man from a nearby village. There would be a great wedding festival in the spring.

"Well, Grandson, the family of the boy who was going to marry your sister came to our house last night. They have decided to cancel the wedding," Grandfather explained.

"Oh no, why?" Naba Raj's heart shrank in pain at hearing about his sister's misfortune.

"I am sorry to say, my grandson, that they think that our family is cursed."

"Grandfather, is this because of my epilepsy?" he asked timidly.

"It may be. Many people in the village think that your sickness comes from the curses of witches and ghosts."

"But Grandfather, the medicine is helping me, and I have very few seizures now."

"We know that, but some others do not understand," Grandfather said. Then he stood up to finish plowing with the oxen.

Sadness enveloped Naba Raj. His epilepsy was causing so much sorrow for the family. He wondered what they were going to do.

Naba Raj, holding his grandfather's hand, continued walking up the hill to the *dhami*'s house. He thought about the effect of his illness on the family.

"Grandfather, will the *dhami* really help Sister today?" he asked.

"Yes," Grandfather said and squeezed Naba Raj's hand to encourage him.

When they arrived at the *dhami*'s house, Naba Raj saw that the familiar steps of *dhami* healing were beginning to take place. All the neighbors and family members were there. The family of his sister's fiancé was also there. Naba Raj wondered how the *dhami* would help his illness and how this would help his sister.

The *dhami* began to shake and talk with the spirits. A chicken was killed as usual and eggs were placed at the crossroads. After many hours of shaking and talking with spirits, the *dhami* finally spoke to the large audience:

"The spirits lifted the curse on Naba Raj's family. The boy Naba Raj may continue to have attacks of falling and shaking from time to time, but these are now a gift. They are not a curse. The spirits know Naba Raj's family is virtuous and will not suffer another curse. Naba Raj's attacks were an omen of a lucky family."

Everyone was very surprised to hear what the *dhami* had said. When Naba Raj looked at his father and grandfather, they looked relieved. Naba Raj saw the father of his sister's fiancé approach his own father. They talked for a bit, then smiled and saluted each other with their hands placed together at their chests. Grandfather turned to Naba Raj and said, "I think your sister will be able to get married now." Naba Raj smiled.

The *dhami* came over to Naba Raj and his grandfather. "How are you feeling Naba Raj?" the *dhami* asked.

"Well, thank you. I am happy my sister will be able to marry now," Naba Raj replied.

"There is other good news, too," the *dhami* continued.

Naba Raj looked at his grandfather with a confused expression.

"The spirits have said that you have a special gift. They said that you have the talent to become a *dhami* like me."

Naba Raj startled at these words.

"You are very kind boy; the care you showed for your sister's happiness demonstrates that. Also, you understand sickness. You could be a very good healer and help others feel better. Would you like to be my apprentice?"

Naba Raj was speechless, but when his grandfather gently nudged him, he slowly spoke, "Yes, I would love to be your apprentice."

"Excellent, come back next month and I will begin teaching you," the *dhami* said, placing his hands together to signal good-bye to Naba Raj. But before walking away he added, "Make sure you keep taking your medicine. If you are going to be a *dhami*, you need to take care of yourself!"

"Of course!" Naba Raj replied excitedly.

As Naba Raj walked back to the house, his heart was filled with joy for his sister and excitement at his future. His grandfather turned to him as they descended the hill and said, "I am very proud of you Naba Raj. It makes me happy that you will be carrying on such an important tradition. Sometimes sickness brings us much suffering. But if you can learn from that experience to understand the suffering of others, then that is a great gift."

Naba Raj felt like an important member of his family and his community. He promised himself that he would study hard and be a good and caring healer. From then on, his grandfather always referred to him as "Little *Dhami*."

3

A Brighter Future

Ajay Pillarisetti

"A Brighter Future" tells Hareesh's story of growing up in a slum outside of Mumbai, where making pottery is the primary profession. Hareesh's situation highlights the problem of air pollution in urban slums in India created by the introduction of bhattis, *which increase the amount of smoke in homes and the number of respiratory infections in affected families. Pottery provides subsistence for many families living in this community, and this must be taken into account when considering ways to reduce the smoke generated by kilns. Families cannot live without kilns; instead, they must replace the ones they currently use with a kind that produces less smoke. Air pollution is caused by cars, trains, factories, kilns,* and *wood-burning stoves, among other things. Youth who read this story will be exposed to the many ways of improving air quality.*

Hareesh inhales deeply. He is standing outside his small home but can still smell the sweet, spicy aroma of the chai his mother is making in their kitchen. The air Hareesh breathes in changes often. It feels different when Hareesh goes to school, feels different near the road, feels different when he waits for the bus, feels different inside his friend Kalpesh's house, and feels *really* different when his dad is working outside with their family's *bhatti*. A *bhatti* is a big oven that is used to temper, or harden, pots. When Dad works outside, the air is really black, and it is very hard to breathe. Hareesh shudders silently, remembering his little brother's hacking cough.

Hareesh lives in Kumbharwada, a potter's colony that is part of Mumbai's—and Asia's—largest slum. Entire families in Kumbharwada survive on one hundred rupees a day, just a little more than two American dollars. Years and years ago, Hareesh's great-grandfather moved from Gujarat, a state in the north of India, to Kumbharwada. "Nanaji," as he called his great-grandfather, came to Kumbharwada to work as a fisherman. Back then Kumbharwada was one of Mumbai's great fishing villages, or *koliwadas*.

After years of making enough money to support his family, Hareesh's great-grandfather found himself in a predicament. The local government had decided to dam up the river where the community fished; the water began to dry up and all of the fish started to die. Nanaji and his fellow fisherman watched their community become poorer and poorer; many were forced to beg, and some moved to other areas to find work. Nanaji decided not to leave his home and instead began working as a potter, the only other trade he knew. Since then, each succeeding generation in Hareesh's family has made beautiful pottery that is sold all over India.

For Hareesh, most days begin just before sunrise. As the sun creeps over Kumbharwada's wide lanes, *bhattis*, and small, two-story buildings that serve as both homes and storehouses, Hareesh rushes up a rickety ladder to help his mother transport finished pots. Today's batch is a group of water storage pots—they have a small opening on the top and a little spigot on the bottom. Hareesh is small but strong for his size; he quickly but gently moves the pots downstairs, washes up, and puts on his gray and white uniform. He must get to school in ten minutes!

Kalpesh is one of Hareesh's close friends. He sees Hareesh sprinting to the school building, teases him about being slow, and gets back to work helping his father make pots. His father has today already made around three dozen pots, which are now baking in the midmorning sun. He watches his father take a brick of wet clay and place it on a large wheel. He then spins the wheel with a stick. The wheel has about a one-foot diameter and resembles a navigation wheel from an old ship. His father deftly spins the wheel faster and faster, and then, with both hands, he shapes the clay. He presses down on the top of the wet clay with his thumbs, creating an opening. He uses the outside of his hand to mold the clay into an hourglass-like shape. Kalpesh takes his father's skill for granted; even though Kalpesh is learning to make pottery, he finds it very difficult! He still hasn't perfected the craft, but he is getting much better.

"Kalpesh, *bheta*, take the wheel," says Kalpesh's father. "You must practice making the pots. One day, you will take over for me. One day, you will teach your own children how to make these pots."

"Yes, Papa," Kalpesh says, moving over to the wheel. He places a block of wet clay on the wheel, spins it, and starts forming the clay. Under the watchful gaze of his father, Kalpesh is a little nervous. The first pot comes out beautifully; Kalpesh is relieved! Kalpesh looks up at his beaming father, returns his smile, and gets back to work.

The midday sun shines down on Kumbharwada, baking and hardening the pots Kalpesh and his father have made. Soon, Kalpesh's mother and sisters will apply a bright red dye to the pots to make them look nicer. Then, the pots will be placed in the family *bhatti* and fired for four hours.

Kalpesh awakens from a brief nap on the upper floor of his house. Kalpesh sleeps here, in a small room that serves as both a storage room and a bedroom for him and his siblings. He crawls over to the window and looks out; he sees Hareesh walking toward a *bhatti* with a cricket bat and ball in hand. It is hot outside, probably twenty-seven or twenty-eight degrees centigrade. But Hareesh knows that, despite the heat, most of the kids will play cricket before the firing of pots in the *bhatti* begins. Besides, the heat now pales in comparison to the heat when the pots are being fired!

Kalpesh runs downstairs, grabs an extra ball, and joins the growing crowd of young people outside. He then realizes that the crowd isn't interested in playing cricket—in fact, most of the balls and bats are in a big pile near his family's *bhatti*! The crowd's attention is fixed on two visitors—an oddly dressed outsider and Rajen, who has been helping the community find new ways to fire pots.

Kalpesh and Hareesh work their way to the front of the crowd, pushing and squirming to catch a glimpse of the outsider and to speak with Rajen.

"Rajendra! Who is this? What is he doing here?" asks Hareesh.

"Kalpesh, Hareesh! *Aja!* This is a friend of mine; he is helping us figure out what is in the air. We think it may be why so many of you children have such severe coughs! He's also going to work with us on installing a new kind of *bhatti* that doesn't produce smoke," Rajen explains.

A bhatti *that doesn't produce smoke!* thinks Kalpesh. He can't imagine such a thing—as long as he can remember, there's been a lot of smoke in his community, and a lot of people coughing and rubbing watery eyes. "Rajen, how can a *bhatti* not produce smoke? We have to get it hot to fire the pots, and to get the *bhatti* hot we have to burn cotton and rags!"

"The new *bhatti* uses gas to create the fire. It does produce some smoke—but much less than the traditional *bhatti* we've been using. Santosh," says Rajen, pointing to the stranger, "has come from Delhi to help us design the gas *bhatti* and perform some basic air-quality monitoring in Kumbharwada. How would you like to be his assistant?"

"Really? That would be amazing!" exclaims Kalpesh. "Can Hareesh help us as well?"

"Of course! We needed two helpers—you two will be perfect!"

Kalpesh and Hareesh share a quick smile and begin running off to tell their parents about their good fortunes. "Kalpesh, Hareesh! Come back here in a half hour! Santosh wants to teach you a few things before we get started!" Rajen says, grinning at the two excited youth scampering off in opposite directions.

Later that evening, Kalpesh and Hareesh huddle around a desk; one dim light bulb flickers in the room. The inside of the house is filled with smoke, like it is most nights—it's the same smoke that the *bhatti* produces. Even though the doors and windows to the homes are kept closed while the pots are being fired in the *bhatti*, smoke gets into the house. It creeps through windowsills, door frames, and little openings in the house, sneaking its way in until all the rooms are filled with thick, black air. It takes a long time for it to clear out—and some days it doesn't clear out at all! Most nights, Kalpesh's and Hareesh's eyes water, and they both cough. They know the smoke is bad for them, but they can't escape it—it's everywhere, inside their homes and outside in the lanes of Kumbharwada.

Tonight's a little different though—Kalpesh and Hareesh are really excited and are reviewing what they wrote down from their discussion with Santosh. He told them a lot about how air pollution is created and how it affects human health. Santosh explained that the problem wasn't just in Kumbharwada—it occurred all over the world, from rural America to Belize to China. In fact, he said, millions and millions of people are affected by poor air quality inside and outside of their homes.

Kalpesh found most of what Santosh explained interesting, but he was especially interested in some of the science. He was learning very basic chemistry in class and had heard of some of the gases that Santosh mentioned. He looked over his notes, focusing on the following part that described the different parts of air pollution:

> Air pollution is a combination of dust, droplets, and gases that are harmful to health. There are hundreds, if not thousands, of different kinds of air pollutants, but the two main ones are particulate matter and carbon monoxide. Particulate matter consists of small particles and droplets in the air that vary in size but are all very small. Breathing in particulate matter can cause a runny nose, watery eyes, and a hoarse cough. For people who already have a cough or have asthma or bronchitis, being exposed to particulate matter can make them feel much worse. Carbon monoxide is a gas that is released during burning, or combustion. Carbon monoxide can cause chest pain and a cough. Inhaling too much carbon monoxide can be lethal.

Santosh told Kalpesh and Hareesh that he was mainly concerned about the small particles—or particulate matter—in Kumbharwada. Because the potters burn kerosene-soaked rags and waste cotton, a lot of fine dust gets into the air—and probably causes a lot of severe coughing and breathing problems. Being exposed to this kind of air once in a while was fine, he said, but being exposed to it every day could be very harmful. Hareesh was a little scared by this, but Santosh told him not to worry—together, they would take some measurements and work on building the first gas kiln, which is much cleaner.

Kalpesh yawns, leans back, and decides it is time to go home. Tomorrow, their work will begin in earnest—they will be helping Santosh build the new *bhatti*. They aren't sure exactly what they'll be doing, but they are excited to witness the creation and be part of something new that could help their community.

4

Leilei's Breakfast

Jie Liu

"Leilei's Breakfast" describes Leilei's struggle with food and with his modern Chinese mother. This narrative explores the roles that food and transportation play in the changing lifestyle trends in China. As globalization pervades cities and towns across the globe, going to fast-food restaurants and opting for other less healthy alternatives have become common rituals of daily eating. Economic improvements are driving changing lifestyles and diets. These dietary changes (such as the adoption of Western foods like McDonald's and Kentucky Fried Chicken) are most evident in major urban areas of China, especially in large cities like Beijing and Shanghai.

Leilei has been sitting at the table for twenty-five minutes in an attempt to consume the large breakfast his mother has served him. "Dear, for the last time, you must drink your milk and eat your toast and eggs; you're going to be late for school!" Leilei's mom shouts from her bedroom in their small apartment in the Xicheng District of Beijing. Leilei moves his eggs around on his plate with his fork and looks out the window.

It's still dark outside, and Leilei is preparing for another long school day. He knows that he should eat his breakfast; he will not return home until after dark because of his review courses. Every day Leilei studies for the high school entrance exam so he can attend a good high school, which will pave the way for college and a future career. Leilei's parents, like most parents in China, expect their children to perform well on these exams.

"Mom, why do we eat the same food day after day? The white bread is dry and overprocessed, and the milk is so thin it tastes like water. Tomorrow can we have stuffed buns and rice porridge like Grandma makes me?" Leilei asks, raising his arms above his head with a yawn. Leilei takes a sip of his milk and adds more sugar; it's the only way he can finish the whole glass.

Leilei prefers a traditional Chinese breakfast of rice porridge and stuffed buns, but he only eats it when he visits his grandmother, who lives in a rural area outside of Beijing. He likes the texture of the rice porridge, made of soft rice and water, which he usually doses with sugar. His favorite bread is *shao bing*, long baked buns covered in toasted sesame seeds that are usually split open and filled with a fried egg, or *you tiao*, which literally means "grease stick." On the weekends, Leilei's mother makes *dan bing*, or egg pancakes, made by beating an egg, tossing in some chopped green onions, and frying the egg on a sizzling griddle. Just as the egg becomes firm, a flour tortilla-like pancake is tossed on top of the egg. It gets flipped over a few times before it's folded and chopped up. Leilei loves to eat *dan bing* with a little bit of chili sauce. When he eats at his grandmother's house, she prepares *baozi*, or buns stuffed with chopped cabbage, carrots, and black mushrooms and dipped in soy sauce, because they make a light, healthy breakfast.

Leilei takes another bite of egg because he knows his mom believes that a breakfast of toast and eggs will give him the energy he needs to survive his long day of studies.

"A good breakfast will help you concentrate and think better in class! Eat your eggs and finish your milk, dear," shouts Leilei's mother. "You must eat at least two eggs a day: they are nutritious, and your exams are quickly approaching."

"What makes them nutritious? Isn't one egg enough?" Leilei pleads as he polishes off his second egg.

"They are nutritious because they contain a lot of protein, and protein will help you think better. When I was your age, it was a luxury to have eggs. Few people could afford to eat eggs every day like we do," Leilei's mother says as she remembers what a struggle it was for her family to buy eggs when she was a young girl. Leilei's mother came to Beijing as a young adult and has lived there ever since. Leilei only visits his grandmother on holidays and so doesn't really know what it is like to live in rural China.

"I finished my eggs and am ready for the day, Mom . . . Can I have some money to buy a hamburger for lunch today?"

"You get lunch at school," Leilei's mother says in a huff as she begins to clean the plate Leilei left in the sink.

"I'm so sick of the school food, Mom! Pleeeease; all the kids eat fast food!"

"I gave you money for fast food the day before yesterday. Once a week is plenty for you to eat that food. Fast food will not enhance your mind for exams."

"But all my friends are going to get hamburger and fries today! It's not only the food we like. It's cool to eat at fast-food restaurants!" Leilei stood at the end of the table pleading with droopy eyes that would be difficult for any mother to say "no" to.

"OK, Leilei, but this is the last time you're getting this treat until after your exam next week, and if you get a perfect score on the math test, you can eat fast food with your friends twice a week until the end of the year." *Not again*, thought Leilei. Every time he wanted a new toy or to play computer games at a friend's house or to do something he really wanted to do, his parents always used his grades as leverage.

In Beijing, American fast-food restaurants are popular with Leilei and his friends. Now that a new McDonald's has opened up right next to school, it's easy for Leilei and his friends to eat there. McDonald's food tastes better than the Chinese buns that the school serves for lunch.

Leilei's dad enters the room and takes a piece of toast off the table. "Son, grab your bag, we're late for school!" Leilei's dad drives him from their home in the Xicheng District in west Beijing to the Xuanwu District in the south of the city for school. They drive a half hour every morning in rush-hour traffic to reach the school, but Leilei enjoys the extra time he has with his father. Although Leilei could bike to school like some of his classmates do, his parents think it is unsafe and too physically straining for him to do so, especially when he is facing exams.

Leilei grabs his backpack and runs after his dad downstairs from their fifth-floor apartment to their car. His family bought a car last year. Chinese-produced cars have recently become more affordable for middle-class families living in cities like Beijing, and traffic now consists primarily of cars instead of bikes, creating congestion and pollution. Some people in Beijing joke that major streets resemble moving parking lots! City residents rarely see the blue sky, as the city is surrounded by a layer of heavy smog.

"When I was your age, Leilei, no one in China had his own car. We all took the bus or else biked or walked to school. I used to bike thirty minutes to school and back every day. The roads were filled with bikes, not cars!"

"But don't you like how things are so much more convenient now?" asks Leilei as he looks out the window at the many bike commuters passing by while their car crawls forward.

"Yes, today things are much more convenient, but biking is a different way of life. I miss the way commuting by bike kept me fit. Now, can you see my belly?" Leilei's dad smiles and looks at Leilei as he softly pats his stomach.

"Can you see MY belly?" Leilei asks, playfully imitating his father and patting his own stomach. They approach Yucai Middle School; Leilei's dad pats him on the shoulder and says, "OK, kid, I'll pick you up after your review class at six."

Leilei grabs his backpack, gives his dad a kiss on the cheek, and jumps out of the car. He runs up the steps to his school, and as he opens the door, he spots his best friend, Xiaodong. "Leilei!" Xiaodong shouts from his locker. "Did you hear what we are doing in gym class today? I can't believe this, but they are going to teach us tai chi exercises, just like my grandmother practices! I'm not going to be able to beat you at soccer today!"

Leilei sits impatiently through math and English classes until it is time for physical education. The students quickly file into the class and sit on the floor, noisily awaiting their teacher's announcement. "We are beginning a new section of our physical education today. We will spend the next six weeks learning and perfecting tai chi exercises," says Mrs. Zhao. The children look at each other hesitantly with hidden excitement. Tai chi is a traditional Chinese martial art. In the morning in parks all over the city, many elderly Chinese men and women practice tai chi to better their health. However, tai chi is unfamiliar to the younger generations, owing to the growing popularity of Western sports like soccer, basketball, and baseball.

"The Chinese word 'tai' means 'great,' Mrs. Zhao begins. "'Chi' means 'origin.' And 'chuan' means 'exercise with the hands.' Tai Chi is our martial art that is beneficial to the mind, body, and spirit; energy flows as you move through the movements. It is known to promote health and longevity, which is why our grandmothers and grandfathers practice this art and remain very fit. Today we will practice a slow-motion routine, focusing on our awareness of our balance and what affects it, awareness of the same in others, and appreciation of the practical value in our ability to moderate extremes of behavior and attitude at both mental and physical levels." Leilei looks at Xiaodong with his eyebrows raised inquisitively. Xiaodong jabs Leilei in the ribs, and they continue to listen. By the end of the class, Xiaodong and Leilei have learned a whole set of tai chi movements, and all the students are eager to show their parents when they return home.

❧

By the end of the day, Leilei is exhausted. Leilei sleepily sits down to a dinner of Chinese short ribs, stir-fried mushrooms, and vegetables. Leilei's mother again nags him about his fixation on fast food. "You know Leilei, fast food is not good for you. It may taste great and be popular with your friends, but Chinese food is healthier for you." "Your mom is right," added his father. "We are eager to mimic the Western lifestyle, but there are many things we are losing from our own traditions that are good for us, such as our traditional Chinese food. We eat a great deal of vegetables and soy and fewer meats and fried foods than do Westerners. It is dangerous for your health if you eat more Western foods and don't exercise enough. This concerns me."

Leilei looks at his father and smiles, "I agree. In fact, I learned tai chi at school today, and my teacher recommends we practice every morning before we eat our breakfast. Would you two be interested in practicing with me? Then, Dad, we could bike to school!" Leilei's mother and father look at each other in surprise. His mother quickly turns to him and says, "That sounds like an excellent idea, my dear! How about you teach us the first set of tai chi movements you learned today?"

After they have cleared their plates, Leilei and his parents stand by the window in their little apartment in Beijing practicing tai chi. Leilei is surprised to discover that his parents are skilled in the set he has taught them.

Once they have finished practicing the set three times, Leilei says, "Since tomorrow is Saturday, perhaps we could make *dan bing* for breakfast. We will be eating eggs, and I promise to study for two hours in the morning!" Leilei's mother smiles, saying, "Of course, you and I can make them together. Sometimes I forget that my mother's recipes are just as tasty as scrambled eggs and toast!" Leilei's father catches his eye, and the three of them roll on the floor with laughter.

5

Tuya's Ride

Ember Keighley and Leslie Greene

"Tuya's Ride" is a heroic tale of a sister recognizing the signs of mercury poisoning in her brother and bringing him to the health clinic for treatment. Tuya's story reveals the problems with toxic substances, which contaminate natural resources that humans depend on, such as soil and ground water. Some places like factories and mines emit substances into the environment that could have a detrimental effect on health, causing, for instance, cancer. The water and soil in many towns in the United States have also been contaminated by mining practices, pesticides, and chemical plants.

"When I was your age, our herd was strong. The rains always came early, and we measured the grass in the pastureland with a forearm. The horses rarely died."

Tuya looked into her grandfather's face. He sat on an orange stool that had been painted by her grandmother. The light from the fire in the middle of their small round home, called a *ger*, reflected off his face, which had become the color of a camel's back from herding the animals all his life. He wore a long brown traditional coat, on which symbols of their country, Mongolia, were embroidered in black thread, fastened tightly around his waist with an orange silk cloth. His black leather boots came up to his knees. He had worn them so long it looked as if they could ride a horse on their own. It had been Tuya's grandfather who had first set her on the oldest and most loyal horse in their family's herd when she was three.

"This year the grass will not grow in time to feed the horses. Only the strongest will survive. Now I measure the grass with one finger. Some days I search all day and cannot find grass high enough for our sheep. It has been six years since the rains came on time."

Tuya's father ("*aav*" in Mongolian) always talks about how the earth is shifting, but she has never been sure exactly what he meant. A year ago her family took apart their *ger* and carefully heaped the giant heavy pile of felt and wood poles onto a rickety, borrowed truck. They normally did this twice each year, moving their camp to the mountains or to the flat, open steppe where the livestock could have better grass to eat. But this year was different. Aav said they needed new work to survive, so this time the truck headed to a small village, downstream from a gold mine. Their *ger* has been there ever since. Many families had already moved there to work in the mine. Even more people earned money by collecting the mine's leftovers and selling the gold they found in chunks of dirt and rock from the river. This is what Tuya's father came to do. Now at night she hears the low drone of trucks in the far distance. The bright lights from the mine make the stars blurry and hard to see. It is different here.

Every morning before the sun comes up Tuya watches her *aav* and her older brother Chingbat get ready for work. Aav pulls on a pair of pants and a shirt with buttons up the front. They are covered in ash and dirt that doesn't wash off when Tuya's mother ("*eej*" in Mongolian) scrubs them in the river. Then he and Chingbat pull the big metal pans off their hooks on the wall and strap them to their backs. These are the pans they use to find gold in the river. Her father kisses her mother, and then he and Chingbat step quietly out the door and disappear into the darkness.

Aav and Chingbat return home exhausted as the sun is slipping below the horizon. They hand pans full of dirt and rocks to Eej. She takes the pans from them with both hands and sets to work washing the contents with water from a bucket she has ready. Then she pours a shiny silver liquid called mercury into the pan. When she heats it on the family stove inside the *ger*, part of the mixture disappears into the air. Eventually, the little pieces of gold appear in the pan. Tuya's four-year-old brother, Naran, loves to watch the last part. He always helps Eej collect the gold pieces for Aav to sell.

Now that school is out for the summer, Tuya and her sisters have their own jobs to help the family while Aav and Chingbat are looking for gold. As the sun begins to peek out over the distant mountains, everyone wakes up to milk the goats and horses. Tuya's two sisters stay by the *ger* to watch Naran and to help Eej with chores around the house. Grandfather tells Tuya that the Mongolian people are very special because for hundreds of years they survived by using their animals for everything they needed. They passed these traditions all the way down to Tuya and her brothers and sisters. Now Tuya knows how to make rope from the hair of their horses, which they use to help tie down the folds of sheep felt on the *ger*. Some days she helps Eej make yogurt and cheese from the goat milk from their flock.

Tuya is not very good at staying still to do chores around the house. But she is the best horse rider in the family, and so she tries to remain motionless at home in the hope that Eej will allow her to help her grandfather take the herds out to graze. Grandfather rides one of their strongest horses, a tall palomino with a long white mane and tail. Tuya rides Khar, the fastest horse in the herd. He was born two years after Tuya. Now she is ten, and he is eight. Ever since she began to ride him she has dreamed of being the fastest rider in Mongolia. This year she is finally experienced enough to run in the children's race during the Naadam festival, the national holiday in Mongolia. She dreams of racing in the open field past the other children, one by one, as everyone from the province cheers. When she crosses the finish first she and Khar will be heroes. Everyone will run over to touch Khar's sleek black body. Mongolians believe you will have good luck and strength for the entire year if you touch the winning horse at Naadam. This year her dream might come true.

"Tuya! Make us proud next week at the race!" called Boldmaa as she arranged fresh pieces of sheep meat in the market display. Tuya beamed and waved quickly at her mother's friend before stepping over the threshold into the pharmacy. Today Grandfather was doing the herding alone because Eej had sent her to get medicine for Naran's headache. His head has been hurting all week.

"*Sain bainuu*, Tuya!" The warm, cheerful voice belonged to Dr. Odonoo from the central city in the province, or *aimag*. Tuya guessed she was there to buy medicine for a patient. Sometimes the doctor made the long sixty-kilometer trip over bumpy dirt roads to their village when people needed her help. She came to Tuya's *ger* last winter when she broke her arm skating on the frozen river. "I see your arm has healed nicely," she said with a wink. Tuya smiled and listened curiously as Dr. Odonoo resumed her conversation with the shop-keeper behind the counter.

"It's getting worse, Gana," Dr. Odonoo continued. "Ever since the gold mine was built people have been getting sick. I have seen miners with rashes and blisters from touching the mercury they use. I've been called here to the village four times this month because a miner or his family member has a headache, is dizzy, or has blurry vision because of mercury poisoning. If they keep using it, it could damage their internal organs and make them really sick."

"*Zaa*, you might be onto something," agreed the shopkeeper. "My sister's husband goes through the mine's leftovers to find gold. This spring my sister almost lost her eyesight, and she started acting strangely. I wonder if it was because she cooked the mercury and gold on the stove at home."

Dr. Odonoo nodded solemnly. "It is possible. Even though you can't always see it, tiny pieces of it can be hidden all over miners' houses. It seeps into the river, too, and so it is also very dangerous for people to drink water and eat fish from the river. I'm especially worried about pregnant women, because all the mercury that's now inside the soil and water and fish can hurt their babies."

"Nobody here wants to hurt their families or the land, Doctor Odonoo," Gana replied quietly. "But everyone here needs the money from the gold. This is the only way we know how to do it. I heard that the government made a law against using mercury, but everyone knows the miners are still using it to get the gold out of the rocks. And who knows how much the mining company has dumped into the river. *Khezuu.* It's difficult."

"I understand, Gana. There's no simple solution. But people should know about the ways they can protect themselves. I've also heard there are other ways to get the gold out without using mercury. We need to do something before things get worse."

Tuya gulped. She wanted to ask Dr. Odonoo a million questions, but she kept choking on her words. Instead she just poked a finger at the medicine in the display case and laid money on the counter. She sputtered out "*Bayartai*" to thank the shopkeeper and ran all the way home to tell her family all that she had heard.

"Maybe this is why Naran has been having headaches," Tuya got out between gasps of air. "We have to stop working with gold, Aav! I don't want anyone to get sick," she pleaded.

She saw her father's eyes begin to glisten as he fought back tears. He pulled Tuya onto his lap and smoothed the sweaty hair away from her forehead. "This is troubling information, Tuya, but how can we be sure? I don't want anyone to be sick either, but we cannot afford to stop look-ing for gold just because one person says the mercury is dangerous. We need to be sure first. The money we get for the gold is just too important to this family right now. I hope one day you'll understand. You are too young to worry like this, *minii okhin.* You should not trouble yourself with these difficult grown-up things."

She wanted to argue with him, but she knew it wouldn't do any good. She desperately wanted to do something, but what could a ten-year-old girl possibly do? She felt helpless. That night Tuya squeezed

Naran tightly as she snuggled into the covers next to him, her cheeks still stinging from tears. Ever since the day he was born, she and Naran had been close. She took care of him every night, and they had always shared the bed on the left side of their family's *ger*.

Maybe Naran will be OK, thought Tuya. *Perhaps it was just a headache.* It scared her, though. She lay awake watching the stove's firelight dance across the poles of the roof. The flickering light almost took the shape of a galloping horse, and her worries faded a little as she thought about riding Khar through the fields. She distracted herself with thoughts of next week's Naadam festival: she would eat warm *khuushuur* meat pies and watch her uncle compete in the anklebone game. She finally slept, dreaming about the race.

The next morning, as Tuya and Grandfather rode past the river, she watched the miners sifting through the riverbed with new eyes. Cattle were drinking in the distance. Two boys were gleefully splashing each other in the water. One man sat on the bank with a wooden fishing pole, patiently waiting for that night's supper to bite his line. A lump formed in her throat again as Dr. Odonoo's warnings about the river now competed with the rhythmic gurgling of the current. She looked over to Grandfather. Sometimes just the look on his face or the way his eyes squinted under his hat would hold answers for her. He had already fixed his gaze on her. "I know, Tuya. I know. I can see that you already understand how important the land and the rivers are to our people."

Tuya tried to put the worries out of her head so that she could focus on the race. Now it was only two days away. Khar seemed to be as anxious as Tuya was. He must have sensed that the big race was coming up soon. As they were riding back home that night from herding the sheep, Eej frantically ran out to meet them. Tuya could tell from far away something was wrong, and she galloped ahead to meet her mother.

"Tuya, Naran is very sick," Eej blurted out. "Today he started falling down and bumping into things. He says he is dizzy, and he can't see things right. He has been acting very strangely, and now he can't keep any food down. I think that doctor might be right—it might be the mercury. He must go to the *aimag* hospital right now. You are the fastest rider, Tuya. Can you make it?"

Tuya was scared. She did not know if she could make it. The hospital was almost sixty kilometers away. She did not know anyone who had ever galloped that far before. That was farther than any of the horses ran in the Naadam races. She did not know if Khar could gallop that long. Then Tuya looked at the panic in Eej's eyes. She had never seen her mother like that before. When she looked down, Naran did not look like himself at all. He was confused and in pain.

"Yes. I can make it."

Eej handed Naran to Tuya. She picked up his small body with her left arm, and sat him on Khar's bare back in front of her. Tuya had never seen her little brother like this, and it scared her more. Eej must have seen her fright, and so she gently touched Tuya's leg. "Tuya, you and Khar can save his life."

Then she ran back into the *ger* and came out with something in her hand. It was the blue silk cloth that always lay at the *ger* altar. It was sacred to their family.

"This will keep you safe on your journey." Eej wrapped the cloth tightly around Naran and Tuya, tying his body securely to hers so he would not get hurt in the journey. Then Eej kissed each of them.

"Tuya, the little dipper is here." Grandfather pointed to the sky above her head. "And the North Star is here. Follow it past three sets of mountains and a large open plain. Then you will see the buildings of the *aimag*. The hospital is in the center of town."

"Aren't you coming with me?" Tuya had never traveled there alone, especially not after dark. She didn't know if she could make it.

"I am too slow. We will not make it in time. You must go alone. We will meet you there later." He kissed her and pointed toward the North Star.

Tuya had barely whispered "*Shuu*" when Khar picked his head up and started to canter. He must have sensed the pit of fear and urgency in Tuya's stomach because he quickened his pace and galloped while she steered him north. She had to carefully hold Naran in her left hand and the reins in her right hand to steer, but Khar was taking care of them all. As her arm grew tired she shifted Naran, and Khar instinctively slowed so they would not fall.

Khar was galloping hard. His hooves hit the plain in four determined beats underneath her, and his powerful muscles moved solidly under her thighs. She could feel him straining with each step to keep the pace he had set. Many horses could not gallop half the distance between their village and the *aimag* hospital. They would become too exhausted and collapse. Tuya spoke to Khar softly and asked him to slow so he would not hurt himself, but he felt how nervous she was and kept galloping fast. Then she suddenly remembered the song Grandfather sang to the horses when they were distraught. She sang lowly at first and then used her whole voice. Khar slowed.

They rode for hours across the plains and by the mountains, the night air stinging her face. Her body was exhausted, and she ached from riding and holding Naran. Every time Tuya let herself think about Naran a pit of worry filled her stomach and tears welled up in her eyes. Finally in the distance, she spotted the buildings of the *aimag*. Khar was struggling, and Naran's breathing was slowing. A wave of relief washed over her now that they were finally within sight.

Tuya steered Khar through the streets to the door of the hospital, yelling for help. A young nurse ran out to meet them. Shaking and unsteady, Tuya tried to get off, but her legs collapsed underneath her from exhaustion. The nurse caught the two children in her arms and whisked them inside the hospital.

"Don't worry. We will care for him," the nurse reassured Tuya as she saw her reach for Khar. He was breathing heavily, but with good care Tuya knew he would be alright. No other horse could have made it to the *aimag* as fast as Khar had. She immediately drifted into a heavy sleep.

When she woke up it was early morning, and light was streaming in through the hospital window to the bed where the nurse had carried them. Tuya looked frantically for Naran before she saw him in the bed next to her. Dr. Odonoo was standing over him calmly.

"He had acute mercury poisoning, but he is going to live. It is good that you brought him here as fast as you did," she explained with a reassuring smile.

"It wasn't me. It was Khar," Tuya replied.

Outside the window Tuya heard the sound of hurried hoof beats and looked out to see Grandfather, Aav, and Eej arriving at the hospital on their horses. They must have ridden all night to reach the *aimag* this early in the morning. Before they had all gotten through the door to the hospital room, Tuya blurted out, "He's going to live! They say Naran will be OK." Eej's eyes immediately relaxed at the news. She hugged her daughter for what seemed like an eternity. Aav scooped Naran into his arms, and Naran flashed a smile at his adoring audience. Dr. Odonoo began to talk to Aav and Eej.

"Naran has been exposed to high levels of mercury. I have done everything I can for him, and he is going to live, but I would like to keep monitoring him. There are long-term effects, which can be very serious. He may have damage to his liver and kidney organs, and his brain function may be slightly harmed. It is absolutely essential that you stop using mercury in your home for the health of Naran, all your children, and yourselves. Next week some experts from the capital city will come to teach about safer ways to get gold without using mercury. Will you come to listen to them?"

Aav agreed. "We must try to do things differently now." He and Eej left the room to talk with the doctor alone. When they had finished, Dr. Odonoo came back and placed her hand on Tuya's shoulder, saying cheerfully, "I could use a brave girl like you to help me teach other people about how to protect themselves from mercury. If nobody tells them, and they keep polluting the water and land, many people will become sick, and animals and fish could die." Tuya couldn't contain her smile and sat up straight in her bed, bursting with pride and excitement at the thought of being given such an important job.

With Naran feeling better now, the family all thanked the doctor and left the clinic together. They walked over to see Khar. He was lying down, but he perked his ears up when he recognized Tuya. His big dark eyes shined, signaling to her that he would be alright, but for now he was too weak to stand. Tuya placed her hand gently on his forehead. It looked small on his long face.

It would be days before he was strong enough to walk back to the family *ger*. She knew that if she tried to ride him in the Naadam race it might kill him. Her dream of winning would not come true this year. Suddenly the race, which had been so important to her for so long, didn't matter anymore. Naran was going to live, and Khar was OK.

"My daughter, I know you are upset that you cannot race tomorrow with the other children," said Aav as he studied her face. Tuya looked down at her shoes as he continued. "But you must know that what you did last night makes you a bigger hero than if you won a thousand races. I am more proud of you today than I have ever been." He wiped a grateful tear from his daughter's cheek. "Even before you rode to the doctor you warned us about using mercury. That is how we knew what was wrong with Naran."

"It's OK, Aav. The race doesn't matter." Then she began to tell them all about what Khar did last night and about how brave he was. She barely noticed that several people walking by on the street had also stopped to listen to her story. Tuya was startled midsentence when she looked down and saw these people gently touching Khar's body.

"Aav, what are they . . . ," she started to protest. He smiled and said nothing, as if he knew a secret. One teenage girl gestured eagerly to her mother across the street.

"Come! You should touch this horse, too, for good luck," she called to her mother. "Did you hear? This girl rode in from a village far away last night to save her brother! She rode this horse sixty kilometers, faster than anyone has ridden that distance before!"

Tuya couldn't speak. Grandfather stood beside her, smiling proudly. He wrapped his arm around his granddaughter's shoulders and looked straight into her eyes.

"*Sain bain. Sain bain.* You did well, little one."

6

Lek's Story

Dredge Byung'chu Käng

"Lek's Story" explores the difficulties faced by people living with HIV and AIDS in Thailand. One of the greatest social problems for people infected with HIV is the stigma they endure. Lek is affected by the virus because his father died from AIDS and because his mother suffers from the virus, which makes it hard to earn money. Children are often affected by AIDS by having to care for their siblings after their parents have passed or by having to assist in earning an income for the family.

Taka taka tak. Taka taka tak. Taka taka tak. The chickens ran in all directions as Jet ran after them. Their long black legs glided easily, zigzagging along the ground until they found shelter. One ran under his feet and stopped just below where he was sitting on the platform at the edge of the house. He could see it wobbling its head and then poking out from underneath. Jet could see another chicken's head bobbing under Lek.

Lek's house is raised about eighteen inches off the ground, and that makes it a favorite hideaway for the chickens. They like to disappear into the gardenia bushes, which have puffy white blooms this time of year. In the evenings when there is a gentle breeze, Jet imagines that this is what heaven must smell like: gardenias, jasmine, and a little rain. In the shade where the air is cool, the smell sometimes takes on the scent of vanilla ice cream, Lek's favorite.

Lek is tall for his age. His skin is the color of brown sugar, and his short hair stands up straight like he has been electrocuted, so he looks a little like a comic-book character. Every day, he wears a thin yellow shirt, dark blue shorts that cover the top of his knees, and flip-flops. His meager house is made of bamboo and palms. It is about ten feet long and six feet wide, about the size of a nice bathroom in America. He lives there with both his parents. When all of his family is home, there is just enough space for them to all lie down side by side to sleep. They have a small refrigerator the color of lime sherbet and an electric fan. The cord for the appliances goes out of their house and across the yard to the only house nearby that is made out of cement. Lek's teacher, Miss Poon, lives there. She has a two-story cement house. The first floor is a beautiful garden, and up the stairs on the second floor is where she lives.

Miss Poon has a thermometer at her house. Jet often goes with Lek to look at it. They know that it is really hot when it is over thirty degrees Celsius, or eighty-six degrees Fahrenheit. Every day, Lek and Jet go to look at it; then they look at each other, shrug their shoulders, and say, "*Rawn mahk*" ("very hot"). They also help Miss Poon with her garden. She has lots of plants. Lek and Jet like the plants that live on air and the ones that eat flies. Miss Poon's favorites are orchids. Lek often waters Miss Poon's plants or gives them some fertilizer, and she gives him a *baht*, which is equivalent to a nickel. He drops it in his shirt pocket and then gives it to his mom when he arrives home.

Last year, when other kids his age attended school, Lek walked to a small garage about a mile away. His mother always worried, because part of the walk was along a busy street with big trucks and fast cars. At the garage, he would take newspapers, office paper, or magazines and put them through a shredder. Then he would collect the long, skinny pieces of paper and put them in large plastic sacks. A factory several miles down the road bought the shreds to pack boxes. They made wooden statues that they shipped to stores in America. Lek could make about fifty cents a day if several people dropped off their used paper. Many days, though, he could only make about half that. On those days he would go to his neighbors' houses to see if they had anything for him to do. He picked vegetables, fetched water, gathered firewood, plucked chickens, washed clothes, ironed, cleaned, or delivered packages. Somehow, he always managed to make at least fifty cents a day to help his mother buy food for the family and medicine for his father.

Lek's father, Mr. Nat, used to work at the silk-flower factory. He had made lotus blossoms that were sold in Taiwan and Japan. But two years ago, Mr. Nat became very sick and had to go to the hospital. At the hospital, Mr. Nat found out that he had AIDS. In the last year, he has lost a lot of weight. Twelve-year-old Lek is now bigger than his father, who, at forty, looks more like his grandfather. His hair is going grey. His skin is pale, dry, and tight. It feels hard, like a worm that didn't make it across the sidewalk before the sun came out. Mr. Nat rarely leaves their little house and only sits up when guests come by to see him. He rarely speaks, but you can see him smile when he sits up next to his son.

Lek's mom, Mrs. Nat, is also sick, but she can still work. She leaves in the morning and walks an hour to the small local hospital where she sweeps the floors. The hospital has three rooms that make a V shape. One long room is for people with dengue fever, which is a type of flu contracted from mosquitoes. Many children in Thailand die from it. The other long room is for people with AIDS like Lek's father. There is a square room in between the two long rooms. This room has an office for the doctor and one for the nurses as well as a reception area.

Jet once went to the hospital with Lek's father when he was sick. Lek and Jet put Mr. Nat on a cot they made from bamboo poles and some fabric. Then they carried him to the road. In the village, one woman owned a pickup truck and had a driver. So she sent her driver to pick them up and take them the rest of the way. At the hospital, the nurses put Mr. Nat in a bed, took his temperature and his blood pressure, and made him breathe while the doctor listened to his chest. The doctor asked Mr. Nat about how he was feeling and what was wrong with him. The doctor talked to the nurses briefly. Then he turned to Lek and Jet and said, "Cryptosporidiosis."

Cryptosporidiosis is a parasite that causes diarrhea. Crypto isn't all that dangerous, but people with AIDS can die from diseases that most people wouldn't die from. If they don't take AIDS medicine, their bodies have an even harder time fighting illnesses. You can get crypto in the United States too if you come in contact with animals, food, or water that have the parasite. Almost everyone in Lek's village owns chickens that run around free. Crypto is often spread through animals like chickens.

So when the doctor said "cryptosporidiosis," Jet wasn't surprised, because it is easy to contract when there are a lot of animals around. Lek looked up at Jet and squinted his eyes. "How do you get rid of it?" he asked. The doctor stooped down so he was face to face with Lek and said, "We have medicine for that." He promised Lek that he would be able to handle crypto. Lek just looked at the ground. Jet also looked at the ground, because crypto lives in dirt too. He kept asking himself, "How can we prevent Lek's dad from getting crypto again when he is surrounded by it all the time? When will the hospital get AIDS drugs?"

Mr. Nat did not get better. Lek continued to help his mother by working during the day. Miss Poon was applying to some organizations to get a scholarship for Lek so he could go back to school. Lek wanted to become a doctor to help people with AIDS, and he could only become a doctor if he continued his education. The richest woman in the village, Mrs. Pim, was interested in helping Lek too. Lek helped her take care of her garden and cleaned her well. One of her daughters died of AIDS a year ago. Mrs. Pim, who also knew Lek's mother, said that she would pay for Lek's education if no one else would. So Lek started to study on his own with books that people had given him. Miss Poon checked books out from the school library for him. Lek and Jet would read together in the evenings about different organs and their functions. Their favorite activity was looking at the world map and trying to memorize all the capital cities.

Toward the end of November, Lek grew excited. He was going back to school. In December, there would also be events he was looking forward to. One of his favorite holidays was the king's birthday. There was a fair held at the temple to celebrate. The king's birthday was just a few days after World AIDS Day, so that meant there would be two events in the same week.

On December 1st, everyone in the village went to the school for the World AIDS Day event. Miss Poon opened the event by giving a speech about the theme for it. This year the theme was "Children Affected by AIDS." "We are lucky here in Thailand," Miss Poon began, "because we have family that will take care of us. No child here grows up alone. AIDS has killed many of our family and friends, but as long as there is one adult left in the village, no child will be without a parent. No children will have to fend for themselves." Miss Poon said that she was very proud that people in the village took care of each other. She said that having good hearts made Thai people strong.

Miss Poon then brought five of her students onto the stage. Each one said their name, their age, and how long it had been since their parents died: "Gee, seven, two years." After a child spoke, an adult came up, gave his or her name, described his or her relationship to the child, and said how long he or she had been taking care of the child: "Lae, aunt, two years." Then the people in the audience clapped, and each child received a toy. Lek and Jet sat in the back and watched. Lek said, "They have toys, but I still have my mother."

Miss Poon continued with her speech. "A few years ago, the Ministry of Public Health estimated that 25 percent of adults in this area were infected with HIV, the virus that causes AIDS. Now they say that it is less than 10 percent. With the way that people have been getting sick, it feels more like 50 percent. We even have some children who are getting sick as well, because they were born with HIV. You may only know about your neighbors with AIDS, but I see how AIDS has affected the whole village. That is why I emphasize that you must be very careful and that we must continue to take care of one another."

Miss Poon then took a sheet off a table and pointed to the computer that was underneath. "This was sent to us by a group of Thai people living in San Francisco. The children at school are already learning to use it. Now, they can type faster than me! Times are always changing, and we cannot stop change. That is the first principle of Buddhism. So we must always remember to prepare for the future. And as long as we continue to stand together and help one another, we will always be ready for anything."

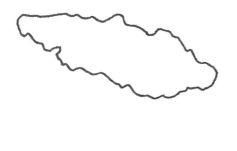
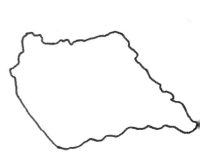

Part 2

OCEANIA

AMERICAN
SAMOA

7

Fa'asamoa
A Sizable Health Problem

Chandra Y. Osborn

"Fa'asamoa: *A Sizable Health Problem*" *describes Iosefo's debilitating struggle with obesity. As diets and lifestyles change around the world, so do the sizes of our bodies. This narrative shows that the epidemic has become so widespread that obesity is commonplace in global society today. It also stresses the health risks of being overweight or obese.*

Each step felt like its own marathon, but Iosefo Atua was determined to reach the top. "It's taken me five times as long this year," he uttered breathlessly to himself as he reached the highest point of the cliff. The gorgeous view of Pago Pago harbor stretched a smile across his plump, round face, masking his slight disappointment about the length of time it took to get there and how exhausted he felt as a result. He quickly rewrapped his sweat-soaked, bright red *lavalava* (a cloth worn around the waist) around his thick thighs before plopping down on the edge of the cliff, lowering his legs off the side. The hot ninety-degree sun melted the perspiration beads on his forehead and wet ring around his face, which remained fixated on the harbor below.

Today was April 17th, known as Flag Day. It was also the day American Samoa became a U.S. territory. It was the biggest national holiday on the South Pacific Islands' calendar. On this day for the last ten years, Iosefo has climbed the same cliff and sat in the same spot, intensely watching the men below prepare the canoes for the Fautasi race (a popular boat race to commemorate Flag Day). Now sixteen years old (and eighty pounds heavier than last year), he remained fascinated with the Fautasi race.

Iosefo grew up in Fagatogo, a village adjacent to Pago Pago (the capital of American Samoa). Pago Pago is filled with colorful semiurban communities and tuna canneries and is home to the unmistakable harbor where the Fautasi race is held every year. Dramatic cliffs surround this harbor, atop one of which Iosefo's large body was now perched. His brown eyes remained glued on the Samoan men below, who were piling into their ninety-two-foot-long boats in preparation for the race. He spent the entire morning motionless, waiting for the race to start, occasionally using the end of his T-shirt to wipe the sweat off his head.

So engrossed in the events on the beach, he barely noticed his little sister, Fa'amata, walk up behind him. She told him to hurry. "*Fa'avave*," she said, adding, "Sefo, Mommy is looking for you!"

Angrily he turned around and snapped "*Fa'atali!*" At that split second he heard what sounded like a foghorn. Someone had blown the conch shell. The race had begun. Fearing the physical punishment if he stayed much longer, with great effort, Iosefo brought himself to his feet with and turned his back to the race. He looked down at his little sister. "Come on Mata," he said. "Let's go home."

Iosefo's large body struggled to keep up with Fa'amata's as she sped back to the village. "Hey, *teine aivao* . . . SLOW DOWN!" he yelled.

She shouted back, "Sefo, I'm not getting a *sasa* because you won't move your *vae puta*. *Savali!*"

After what felt like an eternity, Iosefo spotted their sugarcane-thatched roof off in the distance, peeking out above the banana trees. "Mata, we are close," he said, stopping to catch his breath.

Fa'amata looked back to see her brother bent over and panting. She walked up, laughing and shaking her head. "How do you ever expect to compete in the Fautasi if you can't even walk down a hill?" Fa'amata's giggle was contagious, causing Iosefo's violent chuckle to erupt loudly. His belly shook viciously, as did the phlegm in his chest that triggered a ten-minute coughing session. Then, they started up again.

The remaining fifteen-minute journey was slow, but they walked side by side. They approached their humble *fale* (house), which was situated in the middle of the village. The curved roof was hardly supported by the old wooden posts that surrounded the *paepae* (a raised platform that serves as the foundation of houses in the South Pacific Islands). Between the posts were wall-sized blinds that had been pulled up this morning to let the sun in, exposing the assortment of mats lining the inside floor to its light. Soon, the blinds would be lowered to keep the house cozy and dry during the afternoon downpour.

This April day was hot and humid, like all the others Iosefo remembered. It had begun bright and sunny, and would end with a late afternoon rain, reflecting Iosefo's feeling about Flag Day. At 410 pounds, Iosefo was the most extreme example of an epidemic overtaking most of American Samoa, where at least 75 percent of adults and 30 percent of adolescents are overweight or obese. Few people there have found Iosefo's weight to be a problem because there is a deeply rooted belief that "bigness" is a sign of wealth and power. Culturally, large physical size is a mark of beauty and social status in many Pacific Island countries. Since a high value has historically been placed on being well fed, Samoans continue to maintain a strong etiquette around food (e.g., *never* eat in front of others without sharing, *always* accept and eat the food given to you, handle food with respect, and give it as a gift during celebrations) and remain committed to preparing large quantities of food. Since the Samoan body type tends to be large-framed and muscular, no one had been concerned about Iosefo's size until recently.

Iosefo's mother, Sosephina Atua, was in the *fa'atoaga* (large garden) with the other village women, gathering taro (a yamlike starch), breadfruit (a potato-like starch), and sweet potatoes for the Flag Day feast. Fa'amata ran into the field to assist her mother. Her four other brothers were already outside preparing the *umu* (an above-ground earth oven). Too tired to help them, Iosefo went inside to take a quick nap on a floor mat.

Just then, dark clouds rolled in, as did the heavy rain. Sosephina let out a sharp command. "Go lower the blinds, Mata! Hurry up!"

Fa'amata darted back to the house to find Iosefo lying on the floor inside and gasping for air, with his head slightly elevated above a huge pile of *pua'i* (vomit). "Oh my God, Sefo! What happened? I'll get the boys. Hold on." She bolted out back, where her brothers were tending to the *umu*. "Iosefo can't breathe. He's vomiting. What do we do?"

Her oldest brother, Noah Atua, yelled, "Get the village nurse. Go tell Daddy."

All the family had congregated in the house by the time the nurse arrived. Iosefo's father, Isiah Atua, spoke on behalf of the family, "My daughter found him laid out on the *fala*; he looked like he was dead."

Suspecting his heart was failing, the nurse replied, "Iosefo's condition is well beyond the help of traditional healing and prayer. You must take him to the hospital, so he can be seen by the professional doctors."

Responding in a fashion consistent with Samoan culture, the Atuas asked extended family in the village and abroad to help pay for Iosefo's medical care. The extended family, the *aiga*, is the foundation of *fa'asamoa* (the traditional way of life). All Samoans, even those abroad, support and serve their extended family, often sending significant amounts of money on a moment's notice. This financial support is what kept Iosefo alive at the hospital, where the *palagi* (Anglo) doctors were the first to describe him as "lethally overweight." During that initial two-week stay at the LBJ Tropical Medical Center, Iosefo was diagnosed with congestive heart failure, type 2 diabetes, obstructive sleep apnea, which means he stops breathing at night, and circulation problems with his legs.

It has been one full year since Fa'amata found her brother on the mat, and during this time Iosefo's weight has increased, while his health has steadily declined. On this Flag Day, Iosefo faces challenges much greater than the men who will be competing in the Fautasi race. Iosefo will be fighting for his life—breathlessly exhausted and sprawled out on a hospital bed in the village of Fagalu, near Pago Pago, where the Flag Day festivities will take place. Just like every other year, the sixty thousand estimated inhabitants of American Samoa will commemorate Flag Day with traditional dancing and singing, colorful parades, and the Fautasi race. The island will be sprinkled with American Samoa flags flying from all public buildings, including the LBJ Medical Center. Instead of partaking in these events, Iosefo will spend a second Flag Day in a hospital bed working to get off the ventilator he uses at night and the oxygen he needs all day. He will lay quietly annoyed by the tracheotomy tube lodged in his throat that regulates his breathing. It feels funny, but keeps him alive another day.

Part 3

The
UNITED STATES

8

Overcast Highs

Mary Souder

"Overcast Highs" is a story about Benny, a seventeen-year-old boy who is currently enrolled in a treatment facility for behavioral and emotional health located on the outskirts of Portland, Oregon. Benny's largest obstacle to succeeding has been his inability to manage his depression. His mother, too, has been fighting a battle against depression. Following the example set by his parents, Benny runs into trouble with the law at a young age. He also experiments with drugs and alcohol. It is important to consider that a depressed mood is a common and natural occurrence for individuals according to certain life circumstances. There are many different manifestations of depression; it becomes abnormal only when it regularly interferes with daily functioning.

"GOOOOD MORNING NORTH HALL!" exclaimed an all-too-cheery, especially for 7:00 in the morning, female voice. "'Morning, Benny, time to GET UP!" the staff member enthusiastically shouted as she flicked on the light in Benny's room—a small cement cube that bore an eerie resemblance to the jail cell with which Benny had intermittent encounters throughout the last couple of years.

"Ugh . . . obviously," Benny silently muttered as he turned toward the cold cement wall and threw the covers over his head. He tried to avoid the light that always managed to disregard the shield of his eyelids, piercing the back of his eyeballs with its overzealous energy.

Benny was not fond of light—or any form of energy for that matter. In fact, it irritated him. Energy was something that Benny struggled to understand. One thing that he had acquired an expertise in was feeling sad. This encompassed a lot of other feelings: empty, alone, cold, dark, hollow, black . . . the list went on and on.

"Let's go, Benny, out of bed! Wake up time was ten minutes ago! You now have only eight minutes to complete your morning routine. Don't want to be late for breakfast!" Ms. Erickson scolded.

Benny let out a loud sigh and wiggled his feet slightly to signal to Ms. Erickson that he had heard her. *Darn her for making me realize that I'm still alive*, Benny thought with much resentment as he opened his eyes and gazed up at the bulletin board bolted to the wall above his bed. He saw the "Playful Puppies" calendar and several laminated sheets of paper laden with facility rules. Today was April 1st—exactly two months since the day Benny was transferred from the psychiatric ward to this treatment facility for . . . For what? *Criminals. Delinquents . . . People like me.*

Last December was when Benny got into trouble. He blacked out and does not remember the incident. He does remember that it was just after Christmas. He had bought a large bag of marijuana. Two days later, on his birthday, Benny stole a bottle of his mother's Jack Daniels. *Happy birthday to ME*, thought Benny as he took a long swig from the bottle, which he followed immediately with an extensive drag from his cigarette.

Benny was currently facing arson, minor in possession, and theft charges. He had to fulfill his parole requirements in order to get the charges revoked. Benny wondered how he would ever get through treatment. He felt lost without the drugs, but he knew that he needed to start working if he wanted to stay out of detention.

Benny shuffled to his door, cracking it slightly to allow just enough room to poke his head into the hallway. "Nice April Fools' joke; I'm going back to bed," stated Benny.

"HA!" blurted Mr. Blakey. Benny realized that Ms. Erickson had left the hallway but did not care to inquire as to her whereabouts. Mr. Blakey's expression quickly softened as he saw that Benny's facial expression remained blank. He wasn't kidding. "No, Benny, it's really time to get up," Mr. Blakey blithely replied.

Benny shut his door halfway through Mr. Blakey's undesired but predictable response and returned to his bed, nestling himself under the covers. Still warm. He dreaded the day ahead and shuffled through the prearranged excuses in his mind, wondering if he could recycle any of them in order to avoid his "treatment," as the counselors so fondly referred to it. *Treatment (noun): see "torture."* Benny dozed as he wondered if things could get worse and if he could muster up enough energy to follow through with the plans he had previously made to end his life. *Empty. Dead. Tired. Dark. What could be worse?* Benny considered once more as he drifted back into sleep.

There is a long history of depression in Benny's family. He remembers his childhood. He remembers listening to his father yell at his mother over small things—about supper being too cold or about the soap scum on the wine glasses. Benny would watch while his mother sat in silence and stared at the floor. She always seemed sad, but after these one-sided arguments she would be especially sad. Benny was often left alone, since his mom never wanted to play and since his dad was gone working all of the time. His father's yelling scared Benny, and he soon found himself polishing the dishes free of spots in order to satisfy his father. While he polished he would imagine that each little spot represented a complaint that his father had. His thoughts often drifted to memories of his mom's struggles.

"A vegetable?" Benny questioned.

"No, *vegetative.* Your mother is experiencing vegetative symptoms of depression," explained Ms. Margoff, the treatment facility's psychologist.

"Vegetables are gross," Benny responded, as he attempted to maintain ignorance, but he knew what was really going on. His mother had "gotten bad again," "gone off the deep end"—in other words, she was so depressed she couldn't bring herself to do anything. Not one thing.

Benny's heart would sink as he thought about his mom. He knew how it was to be depressed and felt guilty that he couldn't care for his mom. For a long time he had secretly hoped that his family could end up being happy, but this hope had ultimately become a fantasy.

"Benny?" cooed a gentle voice.

Benny opened his eyes slowly to see Mr. Blakey standing in his doorway.

"Still in bed?"

Benny knew that it was time to get up long ago. He could feel his heart begin to race as he thought about the consequences for holding everyone up. Benny quietly shamed himself—*Selfish! Irresponsible!* He tried to think of more words that people had used to describe his actions. Benny began to burn with frustration. He wasn't trying to be a pain, but he didn't know what else to do!

"What's goin' on buddy?" asked Mr. Blakey.

Benny looked at Mr. Blakey standing alone in his doorway. It was quiet. Benny inquired, "Where is everyone?"

"They already left for breakfast. You're not in trouble—you just need to get out of bed so we can talk about what's going on with you," Mr. Blakey stated softly before he closed Benny's door.

Alone again. Benny's head began to hurt as he weighed his options. He had been told that it is his choice whether he changed or not. He so badly wanted to stay in bed, but knew that it would be a bad idea. *But how can I just put myself out there? I don't have any friends here. No one understands me.* Benny shuddered with anxious thought. He realized that he was scared—he had lost his compass long ago and didn't know which direction to turn. Benny then remembered what Mr. Blakey had said—he wasn't in trouble. Why would Mr. Blakey want to speak to him?

He thought about the other things he had been told while living at the treatment facility. "I care about you." Benny's stomach fluttered as he allowed himself to consider the many ways he had been supported since he began treatment. He also realized that it was true that changing was up to him. *I wonder if I can do this*, Benny asked himself for the first time. A few minutes passed before Benny begrudgingly rolled over and prepared his feet to come into contact with the cold floor, prepared himself to face a new challenge.

9

Bathroom Numb

Courtney E. Martin

"Bathroom Numb" is about Christina, a privileged teenage girl living in the suburbs of the United States, and addresses the devastating role that eating disorder behavior plays in her life. Many American women and men pass on a legacy of delusional and unhealthy perfectionism—often manifested most obviously in body hatred and obsessive behaviors, like counting calories, exercising excessively, yo-yo dieting, and so forth. In addition to offering an inside look at how many young people cope with the overwhelming pressure to perform and with their being under-equipped to manage their own emotions and others' expectations, this story demonstrates how much time, energy, and money is wasted on "body projects."

Christina sits on the cool tile of the bathroom floor and rests the back of her head against the bathroom stall, staring up at the fluorescent lighting fixture characteristic of all the public spaces in her college dormitory. She is trying to figure out how she ended up here, in this place, in this state of mind where throwing up her measly dinner from the cafeteria downstairs is no longer a choice but an absolute compulsion. As tears begin to collect at the corner of her eyes and spill over onto her cheeks, she traces her way back in time.

The first time she ever purged a meal was when she was just sixteen years old, living in her parents' house, feeling totally overwhelmed by the pressures associated with trying to get into a good college, finding a date for the junior prom, earning As in all of her advanced placement classes, competing hard enough to get the captain spot on the junior varsity soccer team, and on, and on . . .

She sat at the dinner table with her family, picking at a meal of chicken, mixed green salad, and broccoli—something that her grandmother may have cooked from scratch but that her mother picked up from the Super Walmart on the way home, carefully making sure there weren't carbs involved. The fact that the Super Walmart was her mother's favorite store was fitting given that she was a supermom: a partner in her prestigious law firm, the president of the parent-teacher's association at school, a loving wife, an overly involved parent, and always, always impeccably dressed and put together.

Christina often watched her getting ready for work as a young girl and marveled at how much energy it all took. It wasn't just the makeup or the outfits or the grooming or the hour on the exercise bike in the den. It was all of this plus the underlying desire to make all this energy disappear from view—to make it all look effortless.

Christina sat at that dinner table, listening to her mom's barrage of questions and advice—"What did you get on the history test? Who do you hope will ask you to the prom? What are you going to wear? I've heard the new drop-waist dresses are slimming. Any word on who made the soccer team? You should be sure to keep running until the verdict to keep in shape. I've signed you up for an SAT prep course. You have to get your score up at least two hundred points if you want any shot at all at an Ivy League. You do want to get into an Ivy League don't you?"

It was enough to make her want to scream. It was as if every sentence her mom said gave another twist to an internal pressure valve. Christina never felt like enough. Not smart enough. Not athletic enough. And certainly not pretty enough. She felt like she was simply going to explode.

"May I be excused," she quickly said, setting her napkin on the table before she had an answer.

"Sure, honey," said her father, absentmindedly.

"Rob, she hasn't eaten a shred of that dinner," her mom said to her father, obviously annoyed that he overlooked the family rule of eating at least half—and usually no more—of your dinner before retreating into your room for hours of solitary MTV watching.

But it was too late. Christina was already up from the table, pushing in her chair, and heading out of the dining room and up the stairs to her bedroom.

Like so many teenagers in her suburban enclave, Christina had her own bathroom attached to her bedroom. It had been a gift on her twelfth birthday—total autonomy with a remodeled bathroom and her own cell phone. She went inside and closed the door. At first she just stood at the sink and stared at herself in the mirror. *Pimples. Fat face. Bushy eyebrows.* She took off her shirt and stared some more. *Pudgy stomach.* She pulled at it, trying to see what it would look like if she lost ten pounds. *So much better.* She didn't dare take off her shorts. Her thighs were too gross to even consider in the bright light of the bathroom tonight. She was already feeling too anxious.

Instead, she grabbed her toothbrush, turned on the faucet, walked over to the toilet, and knelt on her knees. Her friend Cassandra taught her what to do when she felt too full—all you had to do was tickle the back of your throat with a toothbrush and vomit would come out. "You feel like instantly better," Cassandra had promised. "It is either that or smoke a cigarette, and when your parents are around it's like impossible to do that without getting caught."

Christina stuck the toothbrush tentatively back to her larynx and moved it around. Nothing happened. She leaned back. Did she really want to do this? She wondered. So many girls at her school were already bulimic, seeing the school psychologist, worrying their parents. Some parents were clueless, or at least pretended to be. Some girls chose to starve themselves instead—subsisting entirely off of Diet Coke and frozen yogurt. Christina knew she didn't have the willpower for that.

Suddenly she heard her mom walking down the hallway, yelling at her dad: "I just don't understand why you insist on undermining my authority in front of the girls. Christina needs to learn discipline, and instead you are constantly coddling her. The world is tough, Rob, in case you didn't notice. She's got to figure out how to achieve despite adversity."

Anxiety welled up in Christina again, the internal pressure valve twisted hard by her mom's insensitive words. Without thinking she stuck the toothbrush further down in her throat with more force and felt her stomach muscles contract as a trickle of putrid smelling bile inched its way up her throat, came out of her mouth, and fell into the toilet. It looked like lunch. She immediately felt the valve loosen, the anxiety disperse. She had a sinking feeling that purging was her new best friend.

At first she tried to resist the impulse. She would be sitting at one of the long, white tables in the cafeteria, sipping seltzer water through a straw, eyeing her best friend's turkey sandwich and mentally counting all the calories, when that familiar feeling of anxiety would come over her. "Christina, are you even listening to what I'm saying?" her friend would ask.

"Of course I'm listening. Go on . . ."

"So I texted him that I would meet him at 5 at . . ."

But Christina was not listening. She was envisioning the clean, white bottom of a toilet and thinking about the way it now symbolized the onset of an irreplaceable calmness that only purging could afford her. She tapped her foot. She curled up the straw at both ends until it was taut with tension, like her dad used to do. "Flick it," she told her friend.

Her friend flicked it with force, causing the straw to make a loud snapping sound as it cracked in half. She kept talking. "So I explained that bagels are basically the devil and he was like 'OK, fatty,' and I kind of liked that because I knew he wouldn't actually call me fat if I was. Except I'm obviously getting fat . . ."

Christina was counting up everything she had consumed since breakfast. Toast with peanut butter. *So fattening! Bad!* Apple. *Does that count as a carb?* Three lollipops. *Does sugar turn to fat?* Seltzer water. *Makes the stomach feel full. Good!*

"Um, Chris, I just called myself fat and you didn't even object. Is there something you need to tell me?"

"Shut up, you're not fat," Christina obediently answered.

"Little late on that one, Chris, but thanks."

"I have to go to the bathroom."

And that was the end of Christina's resistance.

When she'd gotten the fat envelope from the Ivy League school last spring, she'd promised herself that she would stop throwing up. She'd made an absolute vow that she would break her disgusting habit—she wouldn't call it a disease—of vomiting up a meal or two a week and leave behind all the rest of the angst of her adolescence.

But here she was, in college, thousands of miles from her mom's nagging voice, her dad's silent bitterness, her friends' boring, self-absorbed stories, and she was still praying to porcelain gods. Here she was, taking women's studies classes and critiquing sexism, reading about body image and oppression, and she was still caught up in hating her own reflection in the mirror.

Her head knew what was going on. She'd been taken in by her mom's delusional facade of perfection. She'd been overwhelmed by feelings she didn't know how to process healthily. She'd wanted to be seen and, at the most basic, loved. And she'd used purging as a way to quiet her anxiety and numb the pain of watching her mom march on in quiet and desperate exhaustion. She'd used purging in a last-ditch attempt to be effortlessly beautiful.

But there was nothing beautiful about the smell emanating from the toilet or the quiet, empty sadness at the center of her soul. She knew she was made of something more resilient, something more complex, something capable of more emotional maturity than this. She also knew she needed help if she were ever to become her best, most honest, and gloriously flawed self.

10

Dancing between Cleveland and Standing Rock

Lavone G. Bradfield

"Dancing between Cleveland and Standing Rock" tells the story of Sari and Amalee's biracial heritage and reveals that effective health care on American Indian reservations in the United States is wanting. Through their relationship with their cousin Mya, Sari and Amalee learn about their Sioux heritage and the difficulties of life on the reservation. Mya's struggle with diabetes care and treatment shows the problems associated with ineffective health education in underserved areas in the United States.

"Sari, hurry! You can't afford to miss another day of school! Get dressed and get down here to eat breakfast with your sister!"

"I absolutely refuse to go to school today. I don't belong there," Sari said as she begrudgingly slipped into her chair at the breakfast table.

"Why?" asked Amalee. Sari stared indignantly at her bowl of

oatmeal. She then looked at her sister and asked, "Doesn't it bother you? I can't handle the way everyone makes fun of us because of our looks. Our hair is strange and our skin is too light."

"I like being both Native American and African American. Once we receive our acceptance letters to the Cleveland School of the Arts, everything will be different. You are so dramatic, Sari. Just focus on your homework and your dancing for next year."

Amalee has always had a unique perspective about who she is. It's like she could never be discouraged by other people's judgment of what defines her. Sari has always been impressed by her sister's sense of identity and place in the world—even though being biracial has been difficult for her at times. Amalee is also impressed both by her father's identity as a strong black man in Cleveland, which is reinforced by the many Sunday afternoons filled with stories told by their paternal grandmother, and her mother's history of growing up on a Sioux reservation in North Dakota where they visit every summer.

The girls finished their breakfast, grabbed their book bags and lunch boxes, and headed out the door to school. As the girls rushed out the door, they heard their mother speaking in soft tones with Aunt Marie over the phone.

After a long day of school and dance practice, the girls arrived home to find their mother's face full of tension. Their mother looked up at them as they entered the kitchen, and, with her eyes full of tears, she announced, "Girls, we are leaving the day after school lets out for Standing Rock. Your cousin Mya is sick, and Aunt Marie needs us to help her care for her over the summer."

The girls looked at each other and grimaced because, although they visited Standing Rock briefly each summer, they had never spent more than a week at a time there. Nevertheless, two weeks later, Amalee and Sari piled into their mother's station wagon, and they began the drive from Cleveland to Standing Rock for the summer.

"Mom, what are we going to do in Standing Rock for the whole summer?" Sari asked as she rolled the window up and down. Her mother looked at her from the rearview mirror and reassured her.

"Sari," she said, "you'll be surprised. The kids at Standing Rock are not all that different from you. I'm sure you're going to enjoy your summer." Their mother went on to tell the girls stories of her childhood on the Standing Rock reservation. She told them about fried bread that tastes like sweet county fair cakes, juicy buffalo burgers, and tripe soup made of corn, white hominy, and beef.

As her mother finished the delicious story, Sari looked out her window and realized that they were entering Standing Rock. When they pulled into Mya's driveway, Sari felt a pit in her stomach; they had no idea what to expect. Sari and Amalee looked at each other and swallowed. Mya was diagnosed with juvenile diabetes last year, and recently things had taken a turn for the worse.

"Look, Mom! They're here, they're here!" Sari heard Mya yell from the window.

"MYA!" the girls screamed as they jumped from the car and hit the pavement at a sprint. Sari began running toward Mya as their eyes met. Mya slowly closed the door and began to walk toward her cousins. The twins knew immediately that something was different in her step. "It's good to see you Mya! How are you?" the girls squealed together.

Mya looked at her cousins and smiled. "I'm OK. My legs feel weak, but it's nothing really." The twins look at each other bewildered. Aunt Marie must know something is going on, because the girls can see a visible difference in Mya's health.

Once they were inside the house, Mya sat down on the couch with her cousins and began telling them about her illness. "My legs are weak, and I'm scared. Ever since I was diagnosed with juvenile diabetes, I knew I might have problems. I read a pamphlet about the way that I can control it, but it's impossible to eat the things they say to eat. I don't know if there's a relation, but my legs are so weak now." The twins look at each other worriedly. Mya continued, "Ever since I've felt this tingling in my leg, I've feared that I won't be able to dance in the United Tribes Pow Wow. It's been my dream for so long—to dance in it like our mothers did when they were our age. The doctor warned me that if I don't take my insulin every morning and night, I could lose my sense of balance and the feeling in my legs. I could even lose my eyesight! I hate needles, which makes it so hard to take my insulin. I cry every time."

Mya's mother was renowned for her dancing at the United Tribes Pow Wow. She was a jingle dancer when she was younger and had won competitions around the country. Jingle dancers wear dresses made of silk to which are attached several silver bells that make jingling noises. They wear moccasins made of buckskin and dance to a drumbeat that resembles a heartbeat. Mya was a talented jingle dancer too. In fact, Mya had begun to do extremely well in jingle dancing competitions in Standing Rock. She was looking forward to participating in the United Tribes Pow Wow because it was the biggest competition of the year—Mya knew she had a good chance of winning. She could be just like her mother.

Mya continued to discuss her latest jingle dance contest at the local community center. Meanwhile, Amalee was deep in thought. Finally Amalee chimed in, "I grew up listening to Mom describing the pow-wows. Can we go with you? I'd love to see you dance! How long have they been holding the competitions? Forever, I guess . . ."

Mya smiled. "Powwows began in the 1970s when Native Americans were given permission to honor mother earth and father sky, as our elders once did. At powwows, young and old people dance together in traditional, handmade clothing, and we eat delicious Indian tacos. Indian tacos are made with bread that looks like thick pancakes, and they are filled with fried meat, lettuce, tomatoes, and beans. I love these competitions because it's a time when we honor our ancestry. I want to dance to continue the tradition that is so important to our family."

A week after Sari and Amalee's arrival in Standing Rock, Mya was rushed to the hospital due to pain in her left leg. Mya had been hiding an open sore on her leg for a month, which she thought was simply the result of a fall. But she couldn't remember when she had fallen. When the doctor saw Mya, she decided that her left leg needed to be removed. Mya's diabetes damaged her blood circulation, so there wasn't enough blood circulating to her left leg and her sore was infected. The doctor warned Aunt Marie that without removing the leg, Mya could die of an infection such as gangrene. Aunt Marie began to cry uncontrollably. Mya simply turned her head toward the window and closed her eyes.

A week later, the twins' mother and aunt accompanied Mya to the big public hospital in Bismarck, North Dakota, for the surgery. Mya's left leg was amputated half way up her femur. Sari and Amalee stayed in Standing Rock, anxiously awaiting news from their mother.

After the surgery, Amalee and Sari accompanied their mother to Bismarck to pick up Mya and Aunt Marie from the hospital. When they arrived, Mya was waiting in a wheel chair in her room. The girls entered the room. Mya said nothing. She again looked toward the window and, through tears, said, "My dream is never going to come true."

As they drove home, the only noise was the sound of the motor roaring over the rugged highway. All of a sudden, Sari began to cry softly. Amalee angrily pinched Sari's thigh and whispered, "Stop that right now! We must be strong for Mya. I have an idea that will cheer you up."

Once they arrived home, Amalee pushed Mya to the backyard so they could be alone. "Do you believe that spirits can speak to you in your dreams?" she asked. Mya and Sari nodded. "Before we picked you and your mom up from the hospital last night, I saw your father, Mya. Your father looked me in the eye and said that Sari and I will learn to dance for the United Tribes Pow Wow. We will dance in your honor."

Sari looked at Amalee in disbelief. "But the competition is three months away, and Mya has been practicing these moves her whole life! We can't possibly learn enough to win the grand prize! Who's going to make our costumes?" Amalee grinned at Sari, and then they both looked at Mya. Mya's eyes were again filled with tears; she quietly looked up at her cousins and nodded.

For the rest of the summer, Amalee and Sari danced every spare second they could find. If they weren't eating or sleeping, they were dancing. Mya became their teacher. She showed them tapes from previous competitions so they could learn about the different dances. Sari practiced the traditional dance and Amalee the jingle dance. Since Sari was performing the traditional dance, she would wear a dress made of smooth buckskin decorated with colorful beads and animal furs. To honor Mya, Amalee would wear Mya's dress made of purple silk and silver jingle bells.

Sari awoke early on the day of the United Tribes Pow Wow to practice her moves. As they dressed, Amalee and Sari tiptoed around Mya because she was still sleeping. When they were almost ready, Sari touched Mya's shoulder to wake her, but she didn't move. Horrified, Amalee screamed, "Mom, Auntie, get here quick, it's Mya!" Aunt Marie ran up the stairs. "What's going on girls? Where is Mya?"

"She won't get up! We've been shaking her and she won't wake up!" Sari cried. "Mya! Mya! Please, sweetie, get up!" Aunt Marie screamed. "Get her in the car, we've got to get her to the hospital!" Aunt Marie scooped Mya up in her arms like she was a feather and ran to the car. Sari and Amalee climbed in behind where Mya lay, and their mother jumped into the driver's seat.

When they reached the hospital, the doctors whisked her away immediately. Aunt Marie was upset and couldn't stop crying. They wouldn't let her see Mya. Sari and Amalee felt helpless.

"Doctor, tell me what is wrong with my daughter?" demanded Aunt Marie.

"Ms. Greybull, it appears that Mya's glucose levels were too high— has she been taking her insulin?" asked Dr. Johnson.

"Of course, Doc, she takes it twice a day. She tells me . . . " said Aunt Marie.

"Mya's blood sugar levels were so high that she fell into a slight coma. When young patients learn to inject insulin themselves and do not watch their diets, this can happen. Often children feel withdrawn and just want to be like the other kids. Sometimes they think it's OK to skip their insulin, but it often results in critical situations. I will refer Mya to a nurse and dietician in town to help her manage her insulin and her diet. We have revived her, so you can see her now, Ms. Greybull."

Aunt Marie went to see Mya. Five minutes later, Aunt Marie returned and said, "Mya wants you to go to the powwow right away; she wants you to dance and win the prize money. She said to tell you that she will be there in spirit, even if she cannot be in the crowd."

Amalee and Sari's mother whisked them out of the hospital and into the car so they would not miss the powwow. As the girls lined up to enter the dance arena, Sari began to feel scared. She couldn't keep her mind off of Mya.

When the music began to play, Sari took a deep breath and started to move. She lost herself in the music. Her moves became a part of her, and she felt as though she had been performing this dance for years and years; she had found a new body consciousness, her new dance. After she struck her last pose, all Sari could think of was Mya.

After the United Tribes Pow Wow, they rushed back to the hospital to see Mya. When they arrived at the hospital, Aunt Marie let the girls into Mya's room. Amalee and Sari ran into Mya's room and saw her looking healthy—she was smiling.

Amalee grabbed Mya's hand and said, "Mya! Here is the first place trophy for the jingle and traditional dancing competitions!" Mya's eyes swelled with tears as they hugged her from each side and placed the trophies on her hospital bed.

The next day, Mya was released from the hospital and Sari and Amalee returned to Cleveland. When they returned to school, Amalee and Sari incorporated their new dance moves into a unique dance that no one had ever seen! They marched like the traditional dancers at the Indian powwow. They swayed their bodies from side to side like they learned for the jingle dance, using their favorite R&B song. The judges were very impressed by their creativity and not only awarded them the prize in their school's competition but also recognized them as having choreographed the most unique dance in the whole school!

Over the next two years, Amalee and Sari won the traditional dance and jingle dance competitions at the United Tribes Pow Wow. They also continued to go to Mya for advice about perfecting their dance. Mya was healthier now; with the help of additional education and practice injecting her insulin, she had learned how to control her diabetes. Now Aunt Marie and Mya often volunteered at the Indian health clinic, educating people about the risk factors for and symptoms of diabetes.

Amalee and Sari will forever admire Mya's strength and the way she was able to teach them traditional dance. However, the most important lesson they learned during the summer they spent in Standing Rock was how to be proud of their unique family history and heritage.

11

Joey and the Rain

Ryan A. Brown

"Joey and the Rain" is a story about a young boy living in the Appalachian mountains of North Carolina. Both Joey's father and his older brother, Tommy, suffer from addiction to crystal methamphetamine ("meth"), a powerful and cheap drug that is highly addictive and has devastating consequences. Joey's father is in prison because of behaviors linked to meth use, and Joey is afraid he might lose his older brother as well. A worldwide phenomenon, crystal meth use is particularly prevalent in rural areas in the southern United States. Despite stereotypes surrounding its use that suggest meth addicts can't break the habit, recovery and rehabilitation are often possible but take hard work and strong family support.

Joey was twelve years old and he lived in Soco Hollow, deep in the Appalachian mountains of western North Carolina. He lived with his grandfather, who he called "Papaw," and his older brother, Tommy, in a small trailer next to Birch Creek. Papaw began taking care of Joey and Tommy two years ago after their dad was sent to prison and their mom disappeared. Joey tried to understand. He was angry with his mom but decided she probably just couldn't handle the pain.

Joey still remembered the day the police showed up at their house and took his dad away. His father was a tough man, but Joey saw a softer side of him that day. As the police led him out the door, Joey's father locked eyes with him. Joey saw that a big tear had formed in the corner of his father's eye. He thought a lot about that single tear when he needed to feel close to his dad. Now, he only saw his father for a few hours twice a year. When Joey visited his dad in prison, he noticed the tear had been replaced by a faraway look.

Joey's dad had worked as a carpenter, building big houses for the new, wealthy families who were moving into Soco Hollow. Joey's brother now worked the same job, waking up before dawn and driving more than an hour to get to the job site on time. He often worked ten- or twelve-hour days in the hot summer sun and the icy winter mornings. Tommy was sixteen when their dad was taken away to prison, and Papaw said he became "wild" after that. He never finished high school, but the skills his dad had taught him made him a natural for carpentry.

Joey loved Tommy, but he wasn't sure about Tommy's friends. They were loud, and they stayed out late at night. Joey had heard Papaw arguing with Tommy about these friends late one night. He heard Papaw say, "Those are the same guys your dad got messed up with. I don't want that happening to you, son!" When he heard Papaw say that, Joey's heart stopped cold. That couldn't happen; it just *couldn't*.

Despite his recent worries, Joey was sure that today would be a good day. It was Tommy's eighteenth birthday, and Joey and Papaw had spent the whole day picking out a cake. They used what money they had to buy Tommy a new helmet for his motorcycle, new work boots, and an MP3 player. Joey became excited when he thought about the surprise gifts for his brother; he couldn't wait to show his brother how much he loved him.

On this particular Saturday, it was raining the way it only rains in the mountains: relentless and heavy, as if the rain were trying to take the rocky caps off of the high peaks and drive the creek beds deeper and deeper into the hills. Joey sat by the window, waiting for his brother to come home. The rain meant that Tommy didn't have to work, but his friends had picked him up that morning anyway.

Tommy and his friends were restless and anxious that morning. Papaw gave Tommy an angry warning look on his way out the door, saying, "Remember, it's your birthday, son. We love you. Be good, and we'll see you at six, right?"

"Yeah, yeah, Papaw," Tommy had said, his eyes down, his muddy boots already making tracks down the driveway. Now, it was 7:30 PM, and the skies were already darkening from rainy purple to nighttime black. Tommy was nowhere to be seen.

The beat of the rain, drop after drop after drop, seemed to mimic in its rhythm the mix of boredom and anxiety Joey was experiencing. In desperation, Joey turned to Papaw for some entertainment and company, but Papaw had taken his medicine just an hour before. Papaw lay snoring in his rocking chair, not responding. Joey ran to the fridge to check on his brother's cake, making sure it was still there. Then he ran to the window again, peering out into the darkness, hearing the crickets chirp now, as the rain was lifting. It was 10:15, then 11. Joey could barely keep his eyes open. With his eyes still half open, the crickets seemed so loud that he thought maybe he was out in the fields with them.

Joey snapped out of his dream in an instant with the loud screech of tires in the driveway. *Tommy!* he thought as he looked for a clock. *It must be so late . . .* There was *a lot* of noise coming from the car— loud music, yelling, arguing. Joey listened for Tommy's voice in all the clatter.

"Come *on*! Just a few more hours! We'll go down to the river, use up the rest of this meth." Joey's heart almost sank through his shoes when he heard the word "meth." He had heard the words "meth" and "crystal methamphetamine" a lot during the time his dad was on trial.

"No, I gotta go home, OK? You know how it is . . . my brother, my Papaw. It's my birthday, guys. Hey, I hate it too. I'll catch up with you guys later." Joey's heart sank when he heard everyone laughing.

Joey didn't like the way Tommy's voice sounded—quick, annoyed, and aggressive. Joey remembered the last time Tommy came home this late, when Papaw had to kick him out of the house. Tommy wouldn't sleep, and he kept threatening to break down the door or hurt someone.

Did Tommy really hate us that much? Joey thought. *Would he hate his cake and his presents too?*

Joey's heart raced. *OK*, he thought. *Forget the cake, forget it, I just want all of this to stop. I just want it to be peaceful. I just want to sleep. I just want to stay out of his way tonight.* In a split-second decision, Joey ran to his room and turned out the lights and pretended to be fast asleep.

From the driveway, Tommy had already seen the lights inside the house. Once inside, he made his way up to Joey's room. "Whatcha doin', little bro?" Tommy said with a wry smile as he opened the door.

Joey tried to slow down his breathing, keeping the covers pulled over his head. Tommy tapped him on the head, more aggressively than usual, "I said, whatcha doin'?"

Giving in, Joey relaxed his grip on the sheets and slowly opened his eyes. His brother's eyes were red and wide open. Something about the look in Tommy's eyes gave Joey a deep fearful feeling in his stomach.

"Look what I got, little bro!" Tommy said, a gleam in his eye. He reached into the belt of his jeans and pulled out a small, shiny pistol. "Little bro, I am gonna get that guy who stole my money. Wanna come with me?" Tommy grinned.

Joey couldn't believe what he was seeing and hearing. This was his brother's *birthday*. This was supposed to be a good day. Joey had seen a pistol only once before, and that was just before his dad was taken away to prison. His dad had brought one home and was showing it off in just the same way.

Joey's eyes welled with tears as he looked back up at Tommy. With a mixture of fear and anger, he reached out to grab the pistol, shouting, "No! Just don't . . . just stay here! Just go to bed . . . Just, just . . . !"

Tommy's eyes lit up with a mixture of surprise and rage. He tried to grab the pistol away from Joey's little hands, but they just wouldn't let go. His eyes growing wider, Tommy reached his hand back, ready to hit his brother.

Just then, a dark figure loomed in the doorway. It was Papaw. With deep sadness but strength and authority in his voice, he said, "Son, stop! The police are on their way. Just . . . I'm sorry, son . . . Just stop, *now!*"

Joey couldn't bear what he was hearing. This was even worse. *The police?* he thought. *Not the police! They took away my dad, now they are going to take away my brother!* Joey turned to his brother and said, "Get out! Run!!" But something in Papaw's voice just rooted Tommy to the floor. He sat down slowly on the edge of the bed and let the gun slip onto the floor. Unable to look Papaw in the eye, he sat and hung his head in shame.

When the police officers arrived, things were quieter and calmer than Joey expected them to be. He listened in on the conversation from the hallway, wanting to know everything that was happening but too scared and shy to show his face. They talked for a long time, and Joey kept seeing Tommy nodding his head. Later, Joey learned that his brother was going to a rehabilitation facility, where he would be away from his friends, guns, and the crystal meth and other drugs that were keeping him awake for days on end.

After three months, Tommy returned home from rehab. Joey always remembered that day because it was perfect in every way. The sun pierced the clouds just after dawn, throwing its playful light all over the tall grass of Soco Hollow. Birch Creek sang to him that morning as he sat on the porch with Papaw. Even Papaw, who moved so slowly and never seemed to let anything bother him, seemed excited. His foot wouldn't stop tapping the ground as he sat in his rocking chair, waiting for the moment when Tommy would arrive.

When Tommy climbed out of the white van, something about him seemed different. He walked more slowly, and his smile seemed real and relaxed. There was still a sadness in his eyes, but there was a strength, too, that wasn't there before. As he threw his arms around Tommy, Joey could feel the difference in the way his brother hugged him back. Joey felt his heart swell. *This*, he thought, *is what it should feel like to have an older brother.*

Looking up, Joey noticed that Tommy had tears in his eyes. "I love you, little bro," he said. "I'm sorry. Listen, little bro. It's not going to be easy, but it's gonna be better. No more late nights. No more drugs." In shock, all Joey could do was nod his head in agreement as he looked out at the beautiful fields stretching out beyond the porch. Joey knew it would take work, but if they worked together as a family, things would be different now.

Months later, things had changed. Although Tommy continued to spend time with friends, it was a different group. He continued working as a carpenter but joined a different crew and almost always came home directly after work. Most importantly in Joey's eyes, Tommy was an older brother again. That summer, Joey spent every clear night on the porch with his brother, thinking again and again, *My brother is back. My brother is finally back.*

12

Between Cheeseburgers and *Burek*

Refugee Life in America

Ana Croegaert

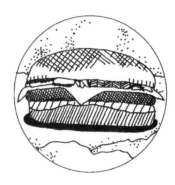

"Between Cheeseburgers and Burek: *Refugee Life in America" is based on the lives of three teenage refugees and focuses on Lejla, a Bosnian refugee living in Chicago. Between 1990 and 2000, an estimated 150,000 people from the former Yugoslavia relocated to the United States. Most of these people were from Bosnia-Herzegovina and Kosovo, and many arrived as war refugees from the Bosnian wars (1992–95) and the Kosovo conflicts that intensified in the late 1990s. The term "refugee" has many different meanings and uses. According to the United Nations High Commissioner for Refugees, refugees are people who cannot stay in their country because their safety is in danger. So, according to the international definition, refugees are people who have a country but are living outside of it because they cannot safely return. In the languages spoken*

in the former Yugoslav state, the word for "refugee" is "izbjeglica/izbjeg-licki" *and is associated with escape, avoidance, and exile.*

Lejla sunk her teeth into the soft bun, slowly slicing through the flaccid pickle, the tomatoes drenched in salty condiments, the shredded lettuce, and, finally, the thin meat patty of her McDonald's cheeseburger. She looked sideways at her friend Sara, who was talking about the boys' basketball game the night before, "Did you see those cheerleaders? Kiana and Lesley think they are so cool, but you know, Kiana's boyfriend is cheating on her—I feel so sorry for her . . ." Lejla listened as Sara droned on about other girls and boys at their high school. She was trying to pay attention to Sara and at the same time keep a close eye on the passersby through the window in front of them. The last time she ate McDonald's, Sami told on her.

Her *majka* (grandmother) was so angry with Lejla when she heard that Lejla had spent money—money!—on that *slaba Americka hrana* (weak American food) that she started yelling and swatting her hand at Lejla. Didn't she understand what good food was? Didn't she know how little money they had brought with them from Bosnia to America? Lejla was tired of hearing about how difficult their life was. Didn't her grandmother understand how easy life could be?

A McDonald's cheeseburger only cost $1.35 and sometimes just 99¢ when there was a special. And it required no work from her grandmother. No mixing pita dough and stretching it so thin across the bed that it looked like a massive bubble-gum bubble that had popped. No stirring the ground beef and onions in the skillet and then carefully spooning a line along the salty, bubble gum-like membrane and rolling it into a tube stretching as long as Lejla's sixty-six inches. No winding the tube into one massive pinwheel and then laying it in a pan coated in cooking oil. No smelling the salty sweetness of the *burek* pie baking as Lejla lay in bed studying her notes from algebra class. No, McDonald's cheeseburgers didn't take that kind of work. Majka could just sit on her chair, unwrapping cheeseburgers: soft little packages representing the ease of American living. Life didn't have to be hard like it was in Bosnia.

Lejla knew this was so because of Jeff and Sally.

Jeff and Sally lived in the same three-story walk-up as did Lejla, Sami, their mom and dad, and their *majka*, their mother's mother. When Jeff and Sally baked chocolate chip cookies, they invited Lejla and Sami to help eat them. Sami would stuff seven cookies in his mouth and four more in his pockets and be heading out their kitchen door before he'd finished chewing, his cheeks swollen like those of a chipmunk who was squirreling away food for the approaching winter. But Lejla would stay. At Jeff and Sally's, the television wasn't on 24-7, streaming in satellite images from postwar Bosnia. There was no risk that walking from the kitchen through the tiny hall to the bathroom she'd be accosted by the virtual image of a wailing mother in Srebrenica, mourning the death of her nineteen-year-old son. There was no chance that Jeff and Sally would start yelling and throwing things at each other after dinner.

When they first arrived in Chicago, her mom and dad had been really happy. They had been separated for eleven months. Lejla, Sami, her mother, and grandmother had been able to leave their town when anti-independence militiamen and citizens had started burning all the homes of people like her parents who did not want Bosnia to become a part of Serbia. Lejla's father had been recruited to remain with the green brigades and defend their region against Serbian occupation. They did not know if he was alive until he arrived in the refugee camp in Istria, just days before they left for America. During the plane ride from Europe to the United States, the family wondered aloud about what their new city—their new home—would be like. What kind of jobs would her mother and father get? What kind of school would Lejla and Sami attend? How would Majka learn to speak English?

At first things went smoothly: Lejla's father and mother attended language classes at the local community college, Lejla and Sami went to school and learned English as well as other subjects with students from Colombia, the Philippines, West Africa, and Ukraine. Majka stayed in their apartment and cooked and watched television. Pretty soon Lejla's parents had to find jobs. They wanted to work—were excited to work—after having spent the past three years in Bosnia out of work because of the war. And they knew their friends and family who relocated to Germany weren't permitted to hold jobs there because of Germany's laws that reserved employment exclusively for German citizens and *gastarbeiter* (guestworkers). Refugees such as Lejla's family were not allowed to work in Germany. But in the United States, refugees could legally work for pay.

Lejla's father got a job at a manufacturing plant, making hinges for refrigerator doors. In Bosnia he had been an operations manager at a shoe factory. Lejla's mother got a job cleaning the rooms at a big hotel. In Bosnia she had studied to be a nurse.

But then the company that her father worked for fired their newest workers, including Lejla's dad. In the meantime, her mother got a different job at a health clinic in their neighborhood. Her mom liked this new job where she was in charge of helping other refugees from Bosnia learn about some of the health services that were available to them in the city. Soon her parents started arguing almost every night. Lejla's father drank more and more beer, and her mother yelled at him. "I can't pay all these bills by myself!" she screamed. "You can't find a job when you are drunk half the time!" Her father would yell back, "This country is horrible! They don't want to hire Bosnians in this country!" and back and forth it would go until her mother threw something—a book, a magazine, once it was a ladle—at her father.

Sometimes her father hit her mother. Lejla remembered her father and mother arguing in Bosnia—sometimes they would even throw things at one another. But she could not remember her father ever hitting her mother in Bosnia.

There was no throwing and hitting at Jeff and Sally's. No broadcasts of dead bodies and crying grandmothers. There was milk and chocolate chip cookies at Jeff and Sally's. Lejla sometimes wished she could live at Jeff and Sally's. Last spring, she and Sami had gotten to live with Jeff and Sally for one whole weekend! Lejla's mother was in the hospital because she had suffered what the doctor called a "brain aneurysm." The doctor said that all the headaches that Lejla's mother had been having had placed stress on one area of her brain and had built a block in one of the blood vessels, and then the block exploded. Lejla's mother had to have emergency surgery and stay in the hospital to recover. Majka and Lejla's father spent the weekend in the hospital with Lejla's mother. So Sami and Lejla stayed with Sally and Jeff. Lejla enjoyed staying with the neighbors. She missed Majka and her father. But part of her wished she didn't have to go back to her apartment and live with them. She knew this was bad—it was wrong not to want to live with her parents and Majka, but she couldn't help it.

After Majka and Lejla's father returned home, Selma, a young woman who also came from Bosnia as a refugee, visited them. Selma invited Lejla and Sami to attend a group with other teenagers who did activities together after school. Sami didn't want to go, but Lejla went. She liked the way Selma's big gray eyes looked at her. She liked the way Selma smiled at her grandmother when Majka invited her to sit and have coffee with them at the small kitchen table. She liked that Selma stayed and laughed with Majka.

All the kids at the community center had arrived in the United States as refugees from Bosnia. Lejla met Emir at the center. Emir lived with his mom and older sister, and sometimes Lejla would go to his apartment and they would eat hot chips and watch *South Park* together. They went to the community center three days a week after school: on two of these days the boys and girls met together, and on the third day, all the girls met together, and all the boys met together.

One afternoon when the boys and girls were together, Selma asked them each to share something with the group that showed how their mom or dad felt about Bosnia. When it was Emir's turn, he said that he hated when his mom talked about Bosnia. "Why?" asked Selma. "Because either she is talking about how perfect everything was before the war or else she is crying—and I know everything wasn't perfect before! And I don't even know why she is crying!"

Selma turned to the others, "I wonder why Emir's mom sometimes cries when she talks about Bosnia."

"Maybe she misses her old home," said Amina.

"Maybe she wishes Bosnia wasn't so far away," offered Mohammed.

"I bet she's mad 'cuz she wanted to stay there longer and fight more so they wouldn't take her house away," Addis chimed in.

"Maybe she feels lonely," Lejla said.

"How could she feel lonely? That's stupid! She has us! We're around all the time!" replied Emir.

"Could you say a little bit more, Lejla, about what you mean about Emir's mother?" asked Selma.

"I mean, maybe she feels a little bit . . . afraid?"

"Afraid of what?"

"Well, maybe she's afraid to be in America. Maybe it seems like life is really hard in America, and she's not really sure how to take it."

Selma told the group that Emir's mother was struggling with a disease called "depression"—that's why she was crying all the time. Selma said that people had different ways of dealing with depression. Sometimes they cried a lot, like Emir's mother. And sometimes when people were depressed they felt a lot of frustration with themselves—and with the people closest to them. They felt angry. Lejla wondered if her parents were depressed. Selma said that when people were depressed, they needed to get help from people they trusted. She said there were adults at the center who could help Emir's mother figure out what she needed. Lejla didn't tell the group that day about her parents' fights or about Majka's obsession with satellite postwar news. But her stomach felt a little bit lighter.

And Lejla began to notice that, even though cooking with her grandma wasn't as fun as baking cookies with Jeff and Sally, when they cooked together, Majka seemed happy. Sometimes she sang *sevdahlinka*—kind of like the American blues—while they stretched the dough thin across the dining room table. Lejla was learning there was a whole world to wonder about and savor between easy, light, fast McDonald's American cheeseburgers and difficult, heavy, slow Bosnian *burek*. Now, when she helped Majka with the *burek* dough, she tried to sing *sevdah* with her grandma. Her mother and father didn't fight so much after her mother's operation, and they would even sing a *sevdah* verse with

Majka sometimes. The songs were sad but hopeful. When you sang them you could show these emotions—sorrow and hope—in how you sang the words, stretching the sounds and changing their shape with your voice. Yes, her parents were angry, and Majka was sad, but Lejla could see that they also had hope.

13

The Cries of a Drum

Alyce Latisha Tucker and Sangogbemi J. Ajamu

"The Cries of a Drum" tells a story about how Jaron, the only member of his family who is HIV negative, learns to deal with the emotional stress and stigma of HIV and AIDS. The risk for HIV infection is increasing rapidly for youth between fifteen to twenty-four years of age, and many youth are currently affected by both the virus and the syndrome. This narrative aims to demonstrate to youth that although they may be struggling with stigma because their parent is HIV positive or coping with the death of a parent, people care about them and there are places to seek help.

"Jaron! You're gonna be late for school again! Boy, you're gonna be late for your own funeral!" LaQuita belts out from the kitchen of their apartment in Atlanta. Her normal voice is sweet and smooth, but today she wants him to know she is serious—her roaring voice cannot be ignored. Jaron is LaQuita's firstborn. "Jaron" means "he will sing or cry out," and he earned his name when he was born bellowing so loud the whole maternity ward at Grady Memorial Hospital could hear him.

Although Jaron's loud voice and strong presence has defined him since day one, he has recently become quiet. Lately, "Speak up, boy!" or "Cat got your tongue?" were expressions frequently uttered in reference to Jaron. His strong sense of self has not disappeared, but he has become more introverted.

Today, getting out of bed is a struggle for Jaron. He rolls off the blue sheets of his twin mattress and pulls the sheets to the bottom of his pillows. He knows he should make his bed the proper way, but today Jaron doesn't have the energy. He opts to face his mother's inevitable irritation.

After Jaron dresses and eats, he races to the corner just in time to meet the school bus, his breath heavy and his heart racing. "Good morning, sir," he mumbles to Mr. Brown, the bus driver, as he climbs the steps. He reaches his favorite seat on the school bus, way in the back on the left hand side, and plops down next to the window. Jaron likes to sit next to the window; the changes in the scenery during the forty-five minute bus ride mesmerize him. As the bus rolls on, his thoughts drift through the events of the past twelve months.

Jaron knew something was wrong when the whispering started last year. His aunts and uncles started saying things like "Quita had to go into the hospital again" or "Look at her, losing all that weight." Whenever Jaron asked his mother what was wrong, she answered, "It's grown folks' business."

When his father died a month later, after a year of battling illness, his mother no longer kept the burning family secret. His mother's words hit him hard. "Your father got HIV from injecting heroin, and he gave it to me. Your two-year-old baby brother was born with it." Jaron had no idea grown folks' business could be so devastating.

Jaron remembers his HIV test and the fear he held inside. He sat with a counselor who explained that a positive test means that you have the HIV virus in your cells, that you have a virus you can never rid yourself of. But, the counselor said, there are treatments. Jaron was ready for the worst. He was ready to fight this virus with his mother. Soon after the HIV test, his life became very confusing. The counselor came into the room with his mother and his mother began, "Jaron, sweetie . . ." He looked up at his mother and saw tears rolling down her cheeks. His mother cried while explaining the results of the test to him. Jaron is HIV negative, and everyone else in his family is HIV positive. "But, Mama, if I'm negative, then maybe they made a mistake about you and my brother." Quita was crying, but her tears were those of joy and relief. "No, baby," she replied. "Your brother and I are HIV positive."

Jaron didn't know how to feel or what to think. One part of him was relieved he was HIV negative because he didn't want to be sick. But another part of him felt overwhelmingly alone. He is HIV negative, which means he is the only member of his immediate family who does not have HIV. Jaron burst into tears, "Mama! I'll be all alone if you both pass away. I can't be alone—I love you so much." LaQuita held her son close to her chest. They sat in silence, sharing their tears.

That was the day Jaron changed. It became hard for him to concentrate in school. He thought at any moment he would come home and find his mother or brother sick. He was angry and felt guilty for being the one that was healthy. It was also hard because his younger brother as the "sick one" got all the attention from the family. They spoiled him with expensive toys and threw parties for him all the time because no one knew how long he would be alive. Jaron's heart hurt. His head hurt, too. How could he be jealous of his sick brother? This jealousy made him feel guilty and ashamed.

Jaron heard some terrible things about HIV and AIDS from his classmates. Some of the students didn't want to touch him or sit with him because they thought he was contagious. They said hurtful things about his mother and father, which only increased his anger and resentment. One kid told him, "Don't touch me—your mama has that AIDS, and I don't want to get sick." Jaron had once been an excellent student, but after his dad died, he had started failing his tests and forgetting to turn in his homework. His whole personality changed. His name, "one who sings or cries out," no longer described him.

When nothing could get worse, something wonderful happened. A teacher at Jaron's school discovered that Jaron's mother and baby brother were HIV positive and that his father had died from AIDS. Finally, all of the failed tests, missing homework, silence, isolation, and sense of shame she noticed in Jaron made sense to her.

With one phone call from his teacher, Jaron's life began to change. "Mrs. Quita, I think Jaron should enroll in a local mentoring program that is for children just like him. It's called Hearts Everywhere Reaching Out or HERO for short. It was designed specifically for children infected by HIV or affected by HIV." The teacher continued, "Through the program, Jaron will be paired with a mentor who will spend time with him once a week. They can go on adventures together and talk freely, without worry, guilt, or shame." LaQuita agreed to enroll her son in the mentoring program and then told him about it.

The first day was the hardest. As Jaron sat opposite this stranger, he repeatedly dipped his french fries in a container of ketchup. "Who's your favorite basketball player?" "Have you seen all of the Harry Potter movies?" "Who is the better singer, Omarion or Marques Houston?" Jaron's new mentor, Derek, tried to break through Jaron's shell and get a conversation going. There was so much that Jaron wanted to say, but he didn't know Derek and wasn't sure if he could trust him.

Jaron wanted to tell Derek that he was angry with his father for making his mother and baby brother sick and angry at God for allowing it to happen. Jaron wanted to tell him that he felt guilty for being healthy and jealous of the attention his little brother received. He wanted to tell him that he no longer cared about anything. But instead, Jaron kept dipping his french fries into the ketchup and letting Derek talk.

After four meetings, they had already created a lot of memories. They watched movies, went to basketball games, and played paintball. Jaron started keeping a journal of his thoughts and feelings. Sometimes, when no one was looking, he wrote rap songs about how he was feeling.

Gradually, Jaron's relationship with Derek went from unfamiliar and awkward to easy and effortless.

By the tenth meeting, they had learned a lot from one another. They had fun together, and, most important, Jaron had someone to talk to. He began to feel like he had support, someone he could learn from. Jaron and Derek discussed hard things and learned from each other. Jaron learned that sickness was one thing and knowing how to deal with it another. He learned that we cannot necessarily control what happens to us, but we can control how we react to what happens to us. He learned that there are good ways of reacting and bad ways of reacting. Jaron knew that he didn't want to choose bad ways, like fighting and causing trouble. He learned that he could deal with anger by hitting a pillow or writing in a journal. He learned that the different emotions he felt were OK.

One day, Jaron told Derek that one of his favorite memories of his father was when he took him to his first football game. It wasn't the actual football game that was memorable, he said, laughing. Rather, it was the band.

Jaron remembered the game as if it was yesterday. "I sat close to my father and peered between the heads of the two men in front of me so I could see the small figures on the massive football field. Halftime was called and the unforgettable happened. A string of uniformed bodies began marching in unison from the sidelines. It was cold and windy; the sunlight reflected off of the shiny brass instruments. In perfect unison, the lines of musicians flowed onto the football field creating an intricate pattern, until the final member reached his position on the field. The conductor's arms rose slowly and dramatically in the air, paused for a brief moment, and then"—Jaron looked up at Derek and saw that he was listening intently, so he continued—". . . shot downward! The sound exploded from the scores of instruments around the field, up through the bleachers, and through the ears and the bodies of all the fans gathered in the stadium! The players were beating their instruments with every ounce of strength in their bodies, and the rhythm ran up through my body and out of my feet and hands. I wanted to dance, to jump up and sing, but I just sat and stared at the drums. Afterward, I asked my dad if I could learn how to be a drummer. I thought I would be a great drummer, but we never had enough money to buy a drum or pay for lessons, because my family's medicines are really expensive." They had reached Jaron's house, and Derek smiled at him as he got out of the car. "See you next week," Jaron said as he slammed the door.

The next week, Derek picked up Jaron and said, "Today, we drum." Jaron couldn't believe it. Derek brought Jaron to his first drumming class, and after the first week of classes, Jaron attended on his own. After a few weeks of class, the instructor noticed his talent and love of drums. He was impressed with Jaron's skill and offered to sell him a drum at a discounted price. Jaron told his mother about this offer, and she said that although money was tight, she would pay for half of the drum if he earned the other half. After weeks of mowing lawns, raking leaves, and washing cars, Jaron finally had saved enough money.

After Jaron slowly and proudly counted the bills and handed them to his instructor, the instructor handed Jaron his very first drum. Jaron beamed with pride and couldn't wait to see Derek so he could show him his new drum. LaQuita was very proud of Jaron, and he knew that his father would have been proud too.

A year later, Jaron performed as a member of a drum and dance ensemble at his school. From the front row, his mother's foot was shaking in anxious anticipation. Derek was there too, with Jaron's little brother. LaQuita could never have prepared herself for what she was about to hear. When it was his turn, Jaron played a solo in which he outshone and outplayed all of the other performers. He cupped, tapped, beat, and slapped that drum with such passion that it seemed like the drum was almost an extension of his own body.

Jaron's music cried out grief for his sick mother and brother. It cried out joy and relief to Derek for his friendship, it cried out thanks to his drum teacher, and it cried out love for his father. Jaron put his whole heart and soul into his music, and he was healing. As the drum ensemble finished their concert, the crowd jumped to their feet in celebration. LaQuita smiled, knowing that Jaron had gotten his voice back.

14

Azúcar en la sangre

Emily Mendenhall and
Elizabeth A. Jacobs

"Azúcar en la sangre" (sugar in the blood) *describes the experience of Irma and her granddaughter Julia when they visit their local county hospital in an urban center. It addresses issues concerning diabetes, depression, and access to quality health care. Irma describes the stress in her life, which she believes increased her risk for diabetes, and her depression. Diabetes has increased enormously in the United States, particularly among Latinos. This narrative explores one woman's struggle with chronic illness.*

Irma sits alone on a blue chair in the waiting room of the county hospital, reading the newest copy of *People Latino*. "Abuelita!" she hears her granddaughter Julia say as she returns from the bathroom in a huff. "I can't believe we have been sitting here for three hours! They took your vitals over an hour ago! We have to be called next; I am sooo bored of waiting."

Julia sits down, and Irma begins patiently stroking her grand-daughter's hair. All of a sudden, a nurse opens the door and yells:

"Irma Gutierez! I—R—M–A—G—U—T—I—E—R—E—Z! Irma Gutierez!"

"Vamanos," Julia says to her grandmother. Now is when Julia is in charge of helping her grandmother communicate.

Irma and Julia make their way to the clinic door and are led to a patient room at the end of the hall. They sit down together and wait again for the doctor. They know that waiting is part of the process, but sometimes they wait so long that it is hard to remain patient.

Irma goes to the county hospital because she does not have private health insurance to cover her medical expenses. She receives support from Medicare, the governmental health insurance for people over sixty-five years of age, which covers most of the costs associated with her diabetes and depression. The medicines are costly, and her poor eyesight and elderly state don't permit her to work.

Irma has diabetes, or, as she calls it, *alta azúcar en la sangre* (too much sugar in the blood). She has to give herself insulin, a medication for diabetics, in the morning and night, to control her diabetes, because her body doesn't respond well enough to the insulin produced by her body. Although Irma finds it difficult to give herself insulin injections, she has persevered through the learning process and is now an expert.

One of the most difficult things for Irma is that she has to live without her favorite foods so that she can better control her diabetes. As a child, Irma grew up eating mostly meats and fried foods, but her new diet includes as many green, red, and yellow vegetables as she can find. Although she has begun eating new foods, she still seasons her broccoli and squash with *picante*. However, the most difficult change she had to make in her diet was eating fewer tortillas. Irma grew up eating tortillas as a girl in Mexico, and to her family, tortilla is the sustenance of life. Today she eats two tortillas a day instead of fourteen, like she did in her early adulthood.

Julia strokes her grandmother's hair as they wait. The nurse they met earlier was extremely kind to them. This was a blessing because the nurses are overworked, and you never know if they will be in a good or bad mood. Today the nurse took time to explain what she was doing and was not bothered speaking through Julia. Because few nurses speak Spanish, Julia often accompanies her grandmother to the hospital to help her navigate "the system" and interpret for her.

Julia sits on the extra chair in the examination room so there is room for the doctor to sit and talk to her grandmother. As they wait, Irma, sitting on the examining table, begins to talk to her granddaughter. "Julia, you know I have had a difficult life," begins Irma.

Julia looks up at her quiet grandmother in surprise. Rarely does her grandmother speak of her childhood. Her ears perk up.

"In the household I grew up in, my mother worked at home, and my father worked in the fields until nightfall. There was little opportunity for me there. I began working when I was twelve years old because we had little to eat. I am glad you will begin high school next year. This makes me proud of you." Irma smiles down from the examining table at her granddaughter. Julia blushes at her grandmother's praise. "I fell in love with your grandfather when I was sixteen, and we married a year later. He lived in the town next to me, and I moved away from my parents. The first year was beautiful.

"We worked hard and fell in love more and more each day. Soon we had our first child, your *tía* Maria. Then things changed. My husband started drinking and was home less and less. After seven years of marriage and four children, my husband left me. You know I am a single woman now, but I was not meant to be. I was helpless at first—clinging to any news of his whereabouts. I searched for news from friends and family. His mother had no idea where he had gone." Irma takes a deep breath and looks sternly at her granddaughter. "Two years later, I received a letter from him, saying he was in the United States, working in Chicago.

"I had no money and four children to feed, so I was troubled about my future. I didn't know what to do because the little money I had from selling the clothing I made at the market barely clothed my four children. I saved every extra peso I could find until I had enough to go and try to reunite with your grandfather. I left two children with my parents and took the eldest two with me."

Julia looks up at her grandmother and smiles. She knows this part of the story well. This is when her mother moved to the United States. "We paid men to help us cross the river. We called them 'coyotes.' I had only thirty dollars left once we reached Texas. Crossing the border was hard; the trip was long and dire." Irma inhales deeply and looks at the ground. Julia knows this is a very difficult thing for her grandmother to talk about. She wonders why her grandmother has brought it up at this time.

"When I finally arrived in Chicago, I had no idea where to look for your grandfather. I finally found him in the Little Village. He had found a new wife, and they were expecting a child." Irma looks away from Julia, and her eyes fill with tears. Julia has never heard this part of the story.

The version she has heard again and again was one in which her grandmother never found her grandfather. Instead, she found a job at a *fabrica*—garment factory in Pilsen, a primarily Mexican neighborhood where many people from her village had moved, and supported her two children. Three years later she paid for her other two children to join her. All four of her children finished high school and college in Chicago. Now her children are married with children and are working to improve the lives of Mexicans in Chicago. Her grandmother is a proud woman, as she should be. Yet, she is surprised to hear this news about her grandfather.

"Once I learned about your grandfather, I was never the same. The shock of his betrayal was overwhelming for me. I began to eat more than I ever did. I gained weight. I worked hard to support my family and even harder to forget my pain. I did not care for myself the way that I should have."

"Abuela, why have you not expressed these pains to me before? I know you have suffered with depression for a long time. Have you ever spoken to anyone of this betrayal?"

"*Mija*, this is something I do not speak of. It is only something I tell you now to explain my illness. The anger I felt toward your grandfather for his betrayal and the stress of this experience gave me diabetes. This is why my health is so poor today."

At that moment, the door opened and the doctor poked his head into the examining room. "*Hola Irma, cómo está Usted?*" asks Dr. Hart. Irma is grateful to be able to speak directly with her doctor in Spanish rather than have to use her granddaughter as an interpreter.

"Welcome back to the clinic, Irma. It's nice to see you again, Julia," says Dr. Hart warmly. "How have you been feeling over the past three months?"

Irma looks up shyly at Dr. Hart. "I have been feeling better, thank you."

Julia, who was very proud of her grandmother's progress, adds, "My *abuela* has changed her diet as you suggested and says she feels much better. On our way to the clinic, we talked about how easy it has become to prepare the foods you suggested last time we were here."

"It is clear from Irma's recent blood tests, specifically her hemoglobin A1c—which, as you know, is a measure of diabetes control, that her health has improved dramatically," said Dr. Hart. "Have you begun exercising like we discussed at your last visit?

Irma closes her eyes for a minute to think. Exercise is harder for Irma to do than changing her diet. She lives near a dangerous street, and this limits Irma's ability to exercise. "I haven't exercised much," she says, looking down at her hands.

Not wanting the doctor to think that her grandmother hasn't done all she can for her diabetes, Julia interrupts. "Our neighborhood is not safe to walk in alone—especially for my grandmother."

Dr. Hart nods knowingly; many of his patients live in similar neighborhoods throughout the city and are hesitant about exercising for the same reason. "Is there an area nearby that your grandmother could get to by bus, or is there a YMCA that she could join where she could exercise? Many of my patients have felt comfortable exercising in their community YMCA."

"Abuela, maybe you would feel comfortable walking in the neighborhood near my school?" suggests Julia. Irma nods in agreement, liking this suggestion. "We could go there together in the morning, and you could easily take the bus home after your walk."

Irma beams at this idea, and Dr. Hart smiles. "Thank you for being so helpful, Julia. It sounds like this is a great solution. It would be best if you could travel together three times a week so that you could get thirty to sixty minutes of exercise on these selected days," explains Dr. Hart.

"Also, before you go," says Dr. Hart. "How is your depression medicine helping you? I know we talked about how discouraged you have felt about your deteriorating eyesight, and the struggles you have had with your weight. If it is not helping you enough, then we can talk about increasing the amount you take or changing the medication."

Irma thinks for a minute and says, "You know, I think it has helped a great deal. I also met with the counselor you suggested; she has helped me work through many things I have kept inside for years. We meet again next week. Meeting with her has helped me feel better about my diabetes and maintain a healthier diet. She is very supportive and understands my struggles with taking my insulin and preparing new foods."

"I am glad you met with the counselor, Irma. Sometimes we all need help to work through things—life experiences can create new challenges we never expected. Visiting with a counselor is a good decision for patients struggling with chronic illness. I am glad you found a counselor who has been able to help you so much."

After examining Irma and making sure her prescriptions are up to date, Dr. Hart says good-bye. "Take care, Irma! Good luck in school, Julia! I will see you in three months!" says Dr. Hart as the two women shuffle out the door.

As they leave the exam room, Julia reflects on how important it is for her grandmother to receive care from a clinic where her doctor speaks her language and understands the special circumstances that make it difficult for her to manage her diabetes.

As the women exit the clinic together hand in hand, Julia looks at her grandmother and nonchalantly says, "I think I want to be a doctor someday. I see how important it is to understand a patient's language and background. I could really make a difference in my community."

As they walk down the street toward the bus stop, Irma looks up through the blazing sun toward her granddaughter and proudly says, "You make everything worthwhile; I am so proud of you."

Part 4
LATIN
AMERICA and the
CARIBBEAN

15

Paola's Tijuana

Elizabeth Burpee

"Paola's Tijuana" tells the story of Elsa and her daughter Paola's life in Tijuana, a border town between the United States and Mexico. Elsa, like many women living in border towns, works in a factory that puts her health at risk. Some factories increase workers' risk for poor health directly by maintaining poor working conditions, and others increase health hazards indirectly by releasing harmful chemicals into the ground, water, and air in the greater community. This narrative also describes the threat that neighborhood violence poses to individual health.

"Mamá! Come help me lift the water!" shouted Paola. The child squatted on the concrete floor, her caramel-colored arms pulling up on the bottom of a twenty-liter clear plastic jug. "Mamá! Come on!" she insisted, grunting for emphasis.

"I'm here," said her mother, Elsa, walking brusquely into the room, wiping her soap-covered hands on the back of her pants. She effortlessly lifted the jug and plopped it upside down on its holding stand. "There," she said, pouring her daughter a glass of water from the plastic monster. "Now go and study."

After finishing the water in three swift gulps, Paola bobbed up and down on the balls of her feet, the first signs of a temper tantrum. "But Mamá, my friends are playing *futból* outside," she whined.

Although Elsa was well aware that Paola had already finished her homework, she was determined to use studying as an excuse to keep her child indoors. The sun was lowering on the dry desert hills of Tijuana, and Elsa knew this was the time when the neighborhood *malcriados* came out. Though the big shot Mexican drug cartels stayed hidden in the cosmopolitan parts of the city, the presence of cheap, easy-to-manufacture drugs kept the streets in Paola's neighborhood unsafe after dark.

Almost every night at dusk, a group of adolescent boys hovered around a spray can. They sniffed any spray can they could get their hands on—usually one they had found in a dump or gutter. About once a week a strange blue van would stop in the neighborhood to trade drugs for small objects the boys had stolen from neighboring homes. Though these boys were often between ten and twelve years old, they successfully terrorized the area with their drug-induced cackles and petty theft. Neighbors tried to shield their families and property as best they could with strong housing materials, but most dwellers in this *colonia* could only afford rotting wood pieces that they hammered together and covered with thin tin roofs. If they were lucky, residents could find used garage doors brought down from California and sold cheap as the outdoor siding of a home. This was hardly a deterrent for the boys, however, when they were high enough to risk breaking and entering neighbors' homes.

A half an hour later, and after Paola had calmed down and successfully read a chapter in her science book for the second time, she and her six-year-old brother Juan piled into their mother's car, ready and eager to drive to their *abuelita's* (grandmother's) house.

"Mom, can you drive to Abuelita's house really fast this time?" Paola asked while her mother started the car, "My teacher told me that I have the best grades in the class, and I can't wait to tell her." With this, Paola felt the car jolt as her mother let out a small yelp.

"*Mi amor!*" Elsa said breathlessly. "That's wonderful." As Elsa pulled out onto the road, her excitement was obvious from the tears in her eyes. Paola giggled and settled into the blissful moment of silence, the car bouncing over small potholes in the dirt road.

Twenty minutes later, Paola opened the door to her *abuelita's* house to find her grandmother lying on the couch, with her long gray hair plopped on the top of her head in a messy bun. Paola ran up and greeted her *abuelita* with a kiss on the cheek. She and Juan played with the two dogs, while her mother made beans, chicken, and tortillas for dinner, and Abuelita napped.

After eating, Paola gave her mother a big hug. It was 6:45 PM, and time for Elsa to leave for her night shift at the factory. Paola hung onto her mother's arm as she pulled away, quickly running her thumb over the red, bumpy patch of skin on the underside of Elsa's wrist.

She looked into her mother's eyes and said, "Mamá, I told you to go to the doctor." Elsa quickly responded, "If God made thirty hour days, then maybe I'd have time to go, *mija.*" Quickly picking up her sweater and walking out the door, Elsa headed to *parque industrial*—the particular factory neighborhood in which she worked.

After Elsa left, Paola couldn't stop thinking about the red rashes that continued to appear on her mother's wrists. *It can't be because of her job*, thought Paola rationally. *She works in the factory cafeteria—not where workers put the televisions together. My mother is proud of where she works; she tells us how her bosses give her bathroom breaks every three hours and how they just installed a new ventilation system so the workers could breath more easily.* Paola knew that these things were important, having heard other women in the neighborhood complain of long hours on their feet, threats from their bosses, and bladder and respiratory problems.

Instead, Elsa's health issues were most likely a result of the area in which she, Paola, and Juan lived. Unfortunately, the particular *parque industrial*, or industry park, that surrounded the family's small community was famous for being one of the most intensely polluted factory areas in all of Tijuana. The fact that the community was nestled in a valley surrounded by factories in the hills above did not help matters.

Worse yet, developers had constructed whole neighborhoods around other factory parks with compact cookie-cutter homes for workers, efficient drainage systems, and paved roads, but not in Paola's neighborhood. Though the same families had inhabited the community for a good ten years, streets were still unpaved, and comprehensive plumbing was nonexistent. Electricity was initialized only a few years earlier, and many homes still had no running water.

When it rained, Paola's mother always yelled for her and Juan to tighten their eyes, close their mouths, and come inside. Once, Elsa had told her children that she feared the rainwater hitting their skin. From inside, Paola and Juan would watch as a small river of green and brown made its way through the creviced dirt road in front of their house. Elsa had told Paola and her brother that it was runoff from the factories in the hills above.

Paola knew it was because of this that her mother had rashes that never went away. It was for the same reason, among various others, that when her mother went to work, she and Juan stayed with her grandmother. Abuelita's neighborhood was safer. Paola's grandparents arrived in Tijuana from the southwestern Mexico state of Michoacán thirty years ago. Her grandfather bounced between factory and construction jobs, while her *abuelita* stayed home raising Paola's mother and her other children. After some years had gone by, her grandfather finally secured his own small ice cream store. By saving as much as they could, Paola's grandparents were able to buy a small house in a bustling part of town with paved roads, a few large stores, and a cathedral.

Paola's mother often told her and Juan stories about grandma pretending to cut off a chicken's head like she used to do on her farm in Michoacán. Abuelita would act as if she were the headless chicken herself, running around flapping her arms, laughing as she bumped into the walls and furniture. "She smiled for a while after we moved to the new house," Elsa would tell her daughter, "but as I grew, the smiles faded and the jokes stopped. It was really hard for your *abuelita* to make friends here, so she mostly stayed at home and cooked all day, waiting for news from Grandpa about when he would return home from work.

"Your grandmother suffers from *tristeza*," Elsa would continue. "She is very sad. Her life used to be filled with fresh air and family, but everything changed when she moved here. I need you to keep her company while I work." "Plus," she would always add, "when you look out of your *abuelita*'s windows, you see hills, not factories."

After her mother left for work, Paola settled into the couch, where she was cornered by her grandmother's massive body on her right and Juan's small sleeping frame on her left. She fell asleep almost instantly but woke to the startling sound of trumpets coming from the television. The credits of a *telenovela* wailed, and Paola tilted her head up to see her grandmother fiddling with the television's remote control.

"Abuelita, I want to . . ." "Shh, *mija*," her grandmother whispered, repeatedly pressing her chubby index finger into the remote with no result. "My favorite soap opera is about to start." Paola could not imagine how her grandmother could differentiate the soap operas she watched all day.

"Abuelita," Paola called sleepily as the old woman got up from the couch to manually change the channel. "I'm first in my class," continued Paola. "Mom's going to register me for middle school next week."

Instead of yelping like her mom did, her grandmother slowly turned around and met Paola with eye contact. "Congratulations," she said with a soft smile, turning back toward the television. As her grandmother changed the channels from one *telenovela* to another, Paola thought she heard her mutter, "So all this has been worth it."

Feeling both proud of herself and sad for her grandmother, Paola peeled herself from the couch and walked into the cool air of a Tijuana night. The last remnants of sunset had completely dissolved from the sky, and the black silhouettes of the desert hills were all that remained visible of the earth. It was usually difficult to see the stars above Tijuana, but unlike her *abuelita*, Paola had never known what the night looked like in the country where there was no constant shine of city lights. Grabbing the wooden fence of her grandmother's house with her right hand and petting the guard dog with her left, she peered through the wooden slats to examine the busy street in front of her.

Some men were standing in front of a small snack store across the street, smoking cigarettes and drinking beer after a long day of work. A little boy made his way up to them with a box of gum, trying to sell it to the men, only to be shooed away. The boy quickly made his way over to the entrance of the next store, jutting the box in front of a woman selling underwear and socks tacked to a bulletin board. On the main street bordering the side of Abuelita's house, families were leaving a megamart with bursting bags in their hands, the children laughing and clutching bottles of Coca-Cola and candy. Cars whizzed by, blaring their music from all parts of Mexico.

Paola stood at the gate for one last minute, taking in the bustling night in front of her. She loved the mix of people, sounds, and smells and could stand behind the gate watching for hours. A car sped by in front of the gate, and Paola finally turned around and skipped back into her grandmother's house to play with Juan and eat the chicken, beans, and tortilla awaiting her.

16

Growing Up Maya

Matthew Dudgeon

"Growing Up Maya" tells the story of Daniel and his brother and the difficult decision his brother makes to migrate to the United States from Guatemala. Hundreds of migrant men and women cross the U.S./Mexico border every day seeking a better economic future. This population shift affects both sending (Latin America) and receiving communities (United States). Some villages in rural Guatemala are void of men and depend on the women for everyday survival. However, the economic lure of the United States has created an expansive exchange of human and economic capital. This narrative also aims to introduce the deeply rich Mayan culture in present-day Guatemala.

Daniel runs as fast as possible up the small dirt path lined by rows of corn whose tall stalks hide the houses located just a few yards from the trail. A cool mist nearly covers the trail, but Daniel knows it by heart. He doesn't know that his grandmother is around the next turn, but he sees her colorful striped skirt and blouse embroidered with roses just in time to slow down.

"Good afternoon, Daniel."

"Good afternoon, Grandmother," says Daniel, returning her formal greeting and trying to appear as respectful as an out-of-breath, slightly disheveled fourteen-year-old boy possibly can. She chuckles and says, "Daniel, you'd better keep running—you don't want to miss your brother Enrique's game, do you?" With a smile Daniel starts running back up the hill.

Women in Daniel's community like his grandmother wear woven skirts of many colors because they are indigenous Maya. They live in Guatemala, a small country in Central America that was once a colony of Spain. Maya lived in Guatemala before the Spanish arrived, and they speak Mayan languages that are very different from the Spanish that is widely spoken in Latin America. The ancestors of the Mayan people built large pyramids of stone that still stand in Guatemala today. Enrique has told Daniel all about the pyramids and how smart the Mayans who built them must have been. He has shown Daniel pictures of some of the carvings from those pyramids, and Daniel was surprised—the faces in the carvings looked just like his father's face and Enrique's face and maybe even his face, too! Enrique has always been very proud to be Maya, and he always talked with Daniel in K'iche', which is the Mayan language that his family and the other families in his community speak. Daniel can speak Spanish too, and in school they only speak Spanish. Sometimes Daniel doesn't understand everything that his mother or father say in K'iche', and sometimes the words are hard for him to say— they are very different from Spanish. But Enrique always helps him—he says that it is important to remember their language.

Enrique has also been teaching Daniel how to work at the loom—he is eight years older than Daniel and has been working at a loom since he was twelve. First the threads—many, many of them—are arranged on the loom running away from where the weaver will sit. The loom pushes some of the threads up and pushes some of the threads down, allowing the weaver to push a piece of wood with thread in it back and forth between them. The weaver can change which threads go up and down with the pedals at his feet. The piece of wood is called the shuttle, and in Spanish it is called *canoa*, or canoe. Once the shuttle has passed all the way through, the weaver presses the threads tightly together with a bar. Shift with the foot, pass the shuttle, SLAM with the bar. Shift, pass, SLAM! Shift, pass, SLAM! Over and over and over again until yards and yards of fabric are woven. Then start all over again.

As the sun is just dipping below the mountains, Daniel arrives at the house where Enrique works—he can hear the weavers working before he can see the house in the mist. Shift, pass, SLAM! The noise, so distinct, helps guide Daniel. Because Daniel is getting old enough to work on the loom more at home, Enrique has been working for don Tomas. Don Tomas owns six looms, while Daniel's father owns two. There are five other young men Enrique's age who work in the same room—all of the looms are clicking and clacking and all of the bars are slamming in unison. The young men are working hard but joking and laughing at the same time, and in the background a radio plays with a fast, bouncy marimba song.

"Hey, little potato," calls out Enrique. "Done with your work at home already? You must really like winding the thread! Maybe don Tomas has some thread here that you can wind, since you like it so much." Enrique smiles as he says this, and the other young men laugh.

"No, Kike," says Daniel. "I don't want more work to do."

"Why?" calls out one of Enrique's friends. "What else are you going to do this afternoon?"

"Pick apples?" says another.

"Gather plums?" says a third.

"Or maybe corn?" says a fourth.

"Nooooo!" cries Daniel. "I want to see the soccer game!"

They all laugh, and then Daniel realizes that they were just teasing him. He laughs with them and heaves a sigh of relief.

"We know, Daniel. We all want to see the game! We're excited, too." Several of the young men will play in the game on Enrique's team. They are good players—one is short, but really fast, and another can kick the ball very far. Kike is an especially good player and has scored many goals. The others are counting on him to help them win the game.

The young men begin quickly putting away their work so they can lock the workshop and walk to the soccer field. Enrique holds back a little, and Daniel waits with him. Enrique slouches over his loom and says to Daniel, "Do you think you know how to use this loom now? Could you weave the way I do?"

"Well," says Daniel, hesitating to answer. Even though he hasn't been working at the bigger looms that long, he is really proud of how well he has been weaving. But of course he knows his brother is much better. "One of these days, maybe. But I am learning, and working hard."

"But you could work the loom, right? Even a big one like this?"

"I guess so . . . sure," Daniel says. Why is his brother asking him these questions?

"You know, part of working the loom is speaking K'iche'. The other guys here, they all speak K'iche' when we're working. So you'll have to keep working on your K'iche', too. Right?"

"Ummm . . . yeah," says Daniel. "Are we going to the game?"

"Definitely," Enrique sighs, putting his arm around his little brother.

Daniel fights the crowd after the game—his brother's team won, and he wants to congratulate Enrique, but there are lots of people around, some of them taking photos. There is even a video camera, which Daniel has never seen before. He crowds behind the screen with some of the other boys, watching the way the camera's small digital screen moves one way while the picture seems to move the other. The camera belongs to don Tomas's son, Umberto. With his many looms, don Tomas is a wealthy man, and he has a television, a car, and a computer. Daniel heard Enrique and don Tomas talking one day about the computer. Enrique told don Tomas that, because computers are relatively new, there was not a word for computer in K'iche'—or at least there wasn't until the Mayans made a new word using old words. In K'iche', a computer is a word weaver, because it weaves words together.

Daniel looks around as he comes out of his reverie, but he cannot see his brother anywhere. It is so strange—he had played very well, scoring several goals. Why isn't he with everyone celebrating?

It is getting late, and Daniel wants to walk home before it gets too dark. Because their community is in the mountains, the sun sets early, as the peaks block the fading light. Daniel knows he'll have to get up early the next day for school, so he starts walking home alone.

The next morning, Daniel wakes up and looks across the room to find that his brother's bed is empty. He wonders where his brother has been all night but doesn't have much time to think about it—he has to get to school. So he walks out to the patio, where the large sink that his mother uses to wash their clothes, the *pila*, is filled with chilly water. He splashes some on his face and runs some water through his hair, shivering a bit when the water hits his head and face, then puts on some clothes and runs a comb through his thick black hair. His mother is in the kitchen, stoking a fire and patting corn dough in her hands, back and forth, pat pat pat, making tortillas that she cooks on a flat, round metal plate, or *comal.* She flattens a ball of dough in her hands, then smooths its edges, then flattens, then smooths, and then places it on the metal plate that is over the fire. The small, flat disks cook until she flips them over with her hands, which are accustomed to the intense heat of the *comal.* Daniel has always wondered how she could flip the tortillas without burning her fingers.

"Daniel," she says, patting a tortilla, laying it down, flipping another, grabbing a ball of dough. "You should look for your brother today after school, at don Tomas's house."

"Sure, Mama," Daniel says, grabbing a stack of tortillas and running out the door to school.

❀

The last few minutes of school Daniel can barely hear anything that the teacher is saying. A hard afternoon rain has been pounding on the metal roof of the school, echoing so loudly that Daniel feels like the sound is filling up the entire room. Finally, the teacher gives up and sends the students home early. Daniel runs to don Tomas's workshop in the pouring rain. He uses his jacket to protect his head, but his shirt and pants are soaking wet.

Rushing into the shop, Daniel looks around for his brother. He looks over to the loom where just yesterday Enrique was weaving, but to his surprise, there is don Tomas working instead. Don Tomas has worked for many years as a weaver, but these days he normally spends more time going to different towns, selling the material woven in his shop. don Tomas sees Daniel come in and motions for him to come over.

"Daniel," he says, loudly, so that Daniel can hear him over the rain, "I have to tell you something. Your brother is not working here anymore. You see, last night he left to go to el Norte. Do you know what el Norte is?"

Daniel knew exactly what el Norte was, but don Tomas's words were only slowly sinking in, so he didn't respond at first. Even if he hadn't been so surprised, he would have let don Tomas explain to him, since he was his elder and a kind, wise man. "Daniel, Enrique has gone to the United States. He left last night, right after the soccer game. He will go to Mexico first, which is a dangerous crossing. He will stay a week or two in Mexico and will learn how to pretend to be Mexican. Then, he will travel up through Mexico, which will take days, or weeks, who knows? Then he will try to cross the border."

Daniel was barely listening to what don Tomas had to say. He was thinking about what he knew about going to el Norte. His cousin had gone a couple of months ago, and for weeks no one knew where he was, and then his family got a phone call saying he was in Houston, Texas. Now he sent money home to his family—Daniel had seen their new cell phone and radio. But Daniel had also heard stories about how much it costs to go to the United States. Young men who wanted to go paid *coyotes*, or guides, sometimes as much as five thousand dollars to take them—a sum that would take three years for a weaver to earn. And Daniel also knew that not everyone who started the trip to el Norte would finish it. He had heard stories about some young men who had been caught in Mexico or crossing the border and who had been returned to Guatemala after being kept in jails for weeks or months. Daniel was scared for his brother and for his family.

"Daniel," says don Tomas, looking him directly in the eye, "I want you to work some here in my workshop. Just for a little while, and just after school or on the weekend. But I want you to learn more about weaving. We could teach you new patterns for you to use on your loom. What do you think? I spoke with your mother, and she agrees that it would be a good idea."

"Don Tomas, as long as it doesn't interfere with my school work, and if my mother says 'yes,' then I will work here."

"And Daniel," says Andres, "we want you to play on our soccer team, too. We know you're young, so you don't have to if you don't want, but . . ."

"I'd really love to play on the soccer team." Daniel is excited, scared, happy, and sad all at once—he'd wanted for so long to play on Enrique's team. Now he would, but without Enrique.

Daniel sits down at the loom where his brother worked just the day before. He runs his hands over the thread in the loom and then begins passing the shuttle back and forth in between them. Back and forth, back and forth, until his thoughts about his brother begin to fade into the pattern of the cloth.

17

The Shaman's Daughter

Dorothy Foster

"The Shaman's Daughter" tells the story of the unique friendship between Mech and Dottie, a relationship that became one of the most important in their lives. Living in rural Guatemala, Dottie was one of the only non-Mam children. This narrative speaks to youth by showing that the bonds of friendship go beyond cultural or religious boundaries.

Dottie first met Mech when she was nine and living on a farm in the misty, cool highlands of Guatemala. Her family had moved to Guatemala, a country just south of Mexico, to work as missionaries in a rural village. Dottie's family lived simply and wore the colorful hand-woven clothes of the Mam people. Her parents invented an alphabet and began writing books in the Mam language. They shared new ideas about farming, medicines, and God with the people in the villages.

In those days, Mam families had few modern amenities like running water and electricity (and today they still don't, for the most part). Much like other people in the community, Mech lived in a hut with a thatched roof. Mech's home was nestled in a cornfield behind Dottie's family's adobe house. Mech and Dottie both came from religious families. Their fathers were both religious leaders, but they believed and practiced different religions. While Dottie's father was a Protestant missionary, Mech's father was a Mam shaman. This religious difference kept them apart at first.

When Dottie's family lived in a hut in the village, she and her brothers would fetch water from a natural spring near the village. The lack of clean, safe water has always been an important issue in parts of Guatemala. The limited supply of safe water is what brought Mech and Dottie together. For many years, everyone carried water from a spring about a mile away to their homes for drinking, cooking, and cleaning. Often, the women and girls carried the water on their heads in traditional heavy clay pots. They spent many hours each day collecting water alone. Dottie and her brothers trudged to the spring every morning, waiting patiently while the water trickled out of the rock. Once they had collected enough water to fill four rectangular tins, they transported it home in their little red wagon. Two of them pushed while the other pulled the full load of water. Bringing the water home was hard work!

This morning ritual continued every day until their small home burned down. They were told that their house was set afire by five angry shamans, including Mech's father, because their church had recently burned to the ground, and they suspected that it had been burned down by Dottie's father's car. There was no evidence that their church had been burned down by Dottie's father shining the car's headlights on their church, as the men declared, but they blamed her father nonetheless. Cars were unknown in the Mam village, and Dottie's family was an anomaly there. The shamans believed that Dottie's parents were a threat to their way of life and income because they were teaching new ideas about God and medicine. They feared new ideas and technology because they were unfamiliar with them.

After Dottie's family's house burned down, they moved into the old farmhouse. Her father arranged to have a pipeline laid from a mountain spring to a *pila*, or open water tank in their yard. Dottie and her brothers were ecstatic because they would no longer have to carry water in their little red wagon. They were the first family in the village to have water piped directly to their house. Soon mothers with children shyly clinging to their skirts began visiting the *pila* to fill their clay pots. The *pila* became a way for Dottie to meet children in the village. Dottie had a curious and kind personality, and she slowly befriended many of the children who accompanied their mothers to the *pila*. The children were curious about her crayons and coloring books. Before long, Dottie was teaching a group of children how to print their ABCs.

One morning, Mech visited the *pila* with her clay pot. Dottie had seen her in the fields, cultivating corn with her father. Mech's father had warned his daughter never to go near Dottie's family. The need for water, however, dampened his apprehension and fear. He was now allowing Mech to visit the *pila*.

Before long, Mech looked over to the table on the porch of Dottie's house, where the children were studying. "*Qlana*," Dottie said to Mech in Mam, asking her to come close. Mech, frightened by Dottie's address, looked up, startled, and hastened out the gate. Gradually, as Mech's visits became more regular, she started coming closer to the table and stayed longer. She wanted to learn more about the sounds and letters in Mam, which Dottie regularly taught to the children.

After two months of visiting the water pump, Mech had become a member of the group. Fear was replaced by trust. Before long, Mech and Dottie became best friends. Mech became Dottie's teacher, correcting her mistakes in Mam. She taught Dottie many secrets of her culture: how to grind corn on a stone *ca*, how to weave on a backstrap loom, how to tend sheep so they wouldn't run away, what to do when a boy gives you his handkerchief. Dottie was happy to know that you don't wash it unless you want to become his wife!

As their friendship grew, Dottie often helped Mech herd her sheep. One day, they herded twenty-five sheep to a green field of grass near the river. When they were about to lead the sheep home, Mech realized that one of the sheep was missing. They searched behind every bush and tree for the little sheep but could not find it. Mech became frightened, knowing that she would be severely beaten when she got home if she and Dottie did not find the lost sheep. For a poor family, the loss of one sheep could mean starvation when they ran out of corn in the dry season.

Ordering her little brother to stay with the sheep, Mech headed toward the steep embankment of the river. Dottie held back, not knowing whether to stay with the sheep or to follow Mech. Peering down, Dottie saw a flash of gray fur and heard a chilling howl. Without hesitation, Mech grabbed a large stick and threw it at the coyote and the growling predator took off downstream. Dottie looked to the middle of the river and saw the sheep was clinging to a rock, bleating. Mech quickly waded up to her waist in the raging current and grabbed the sheep. Dottie ran to the riverbank to help her haul the heavy, wet, and smelly sheep up to safety.

Dottie admired the bravery and dedication to her family that Mech showed when she saved the sheep from the coyote and raging river. She was proud to have a friend like Mech. It was the need for water that brought the girls together and the courage of facing the water in that raging river that cemented their friendship. Mech and Dottie remain best friends after more than sixty-five years, and Mech welcomes Dottie and her family into her home every time they visit. After so many years, they still share much as friends and continue to learn from each other.

18

Students Fight Rubella

Ana Elena Chévez

"Students Fight Rubella" tells the story of students from Santa Sofia School in El Salvador who help in the national rubella vaccination campaign. Vaccines are concoctions developed to provide viral immunity on an individual level, which can then impact the presence of a disease in the community. Viral immunity means that an individual has antibodies to fight off a viral infection. This is important because there are few medicinal cures for viral infections like rubella, mumps, measles, polio, and whooping cough (pertussis). Vaccinations have successfully eradicated diseases like smallpox and polio in parts of the world.

Zoilita sits thoughtfully listening to the principal of the Santa Sofia School during a student assembly. Zoilita lives in San Miguel, which is the western district of El Salvador, a country in Central America. Her ears perk up when she hears, "The students of Santa Sofia School will participate in the national rubella vaccination campaign in February and March. Rubella is a virus that affects the skin and lymph nodes and is transmitted by droplets from the nose or throat that other people breathe."

Zoilita squirms in her seat, trying to squash the fear that comes over her at the thought of needles, remembering her mother's words, "Twelve-year-olds are too old to scream at the site of a needle." Zoilita turns to her best friend, Yolanda, and whispers, "Will we have to be vaccinated? I've heard about vaccinations before, and it sounds like something you're supposed to get when you're young, but I'm not sure what it does." Yolanda's mind has been somewhere else, perhaps on her upcoming test on long division or the cute boy sitting three seats to her right. "Zoilita, I'm not so sure about getting vaccinated—I am so scared of needles!"

Zoilita is an extremely curious girl. She is a dedicated student, active in her class despite being very shy. Today she is particularly interested in her principal's weekly all-school address because she recently discussed vaccines with her mother. Her mother is a health worker and is concerned about the recent rubella outbreak. El Salvador has been successful in vaccinating many children against childhood diseases, but it is a very small country, so an outbreak confined to one area could swiftly travel across the country.

Zoilita slowly raises her hand and then waves it in the air so Mrs. Rodriguez can see her. Mrs. Rodriguez sees her hand, nods toward her, and says, "Yes, Zoilita. Do you have a question?" Zoilita swallows and stands to address the principal. "Mrs. Rodriguez, I would like to know if you want us to be vaccinated during this campaign? And, if you do, what is a vaccine, and what does it do in the body?"

"What good questions, Zoilita. Each of you will be vaccinated during this national campaign, because one can receive the vaccine if one is between the ages eight to thirty-nine. This is an important age group to vaccinate because rubella can affect both children and their parents; mothers pass it along to their babies, which can have harmful results."

Extremely curious, Zoilita interrupts—"But Mrs. Rodriguez, what is the vaccine preventing?" Mrs. Rodriguez smiles and continues, "The vaccine prevents rubella. Rubella is a virus that often causes fever and a rash." Yolanda looks at Zoilita with a grimace because she knows where this is going. Mrs. Rodriguez was a science teacher before she became the principal and always likes to be precise in her descriptions. "A virus is a small particle that infects cells in biological organisms. Viruses can reproduce only by invading and taking over other cells. Therefore, rubella becomes a part of your cells and is very difficult to cure. If you are vaccinated, however, you already have information in your cells to fight the virus—so you cannot become infected with rubella."

The students look at each other and nod, thinking this campaign might not be a bad idea after all.

"If we vaccinate every student in the school and in the whole town, we could eradicate rubella in our town. If we vaccinate all the children in El Salvador, we could prevent all further outbreaks, and our country would be rubella-free!" Mrs. Rodriguez smiled, seeing that the pinnacle of her speech had engaged her students. She continued, "Rubella affects healthy children, who often recover quickly, like you. However, if rubella infects a pregnant woman, then her baby is at risk for malformations. These malformations put the baby's life in danger and can affect him or her during his or her whole life."

Mrs. Rodriguez's explanation concerns Zoilita. Last week, she heard rumors that one of the assistants at Santa Sofia School—who is expecting a baby in three months—was infected with rubella. She looks at Yolanda and notices that she looks concerned and deep in thought. Zoilita feels certain that she heard the same rumors. Yolanda, one of the most outgoing girls in her class, is suddenly tuned in to Mrs. Rodriguez's assembly. She raises her hand and asks, "But what happens if a baby gets rubella?"

"Well, Yolanda, if a pregnant woman has rubella, her baby can be born deaf, blind, and/or have heart problems." This comment generates muffled conversations throughout the room. "Students, we can play an important role in eradicating rubella and becoming a part of the prevention project," asserts Mrs. Rodriguez. "Would you be interested to hear more about rubella from health workers at our local health unit?

Would you be interested in helping with the rubella campaign effort?" The students all begin to chatter, and Mrs. Rodriguez hears a number of yeses ring throughout the assembly hall. She smiles and dismisses the assembly.

After the students file out of the assembly and into their classes, Mrs. Rodriguez closes the door to her office and calls the director of the San Miguel Health Center, a close friend of hers who had offered to make a presentation about the rubella campaign to the students next week. Surprised by her students' overwhelming interest and excitement, Mrs. Rodriguez invites Dr. Chévez to speak to the students.

One week later, Dr. Chévez addresses the students formally at the weekly school assembly. "We will begin the rubella vaccination campaign by vaccinating people who are high risk, such as young people and mothers. We will begin vaccinating all students in public and private schools in San Miguel. We will also vaccinate all of the workers younger than forty years of age in the central commercial district of San Miguel. The weekends are when we will need your help! We will provide rubella vaccinations at churches, parks, and community markets and need you all to take turns helping us recruit your family and friends to get vaccinated! We will need your help for six weeks of the campaign. During the last two weeks of the campaign, we will vaccinate the remaining members of the population in their homes."

"Dr. Chévez," says Yolanda, her hand shooting up into the air. "Yes, dear?" responds Dr. Chévez. "I have already told my family and friends about the campaign and I am trying to learn more about rubella myself, but I want to do more. How can we help?"

"Well, in addition to educating your family and friends, you could also encourage your neighbors to participate in our weekend activities. You should attend them yourselves. Every citizen is an important part of the campaign, especially exemplary students from Santa Sofia School!" says Dr. Chévez.

At the end of Dr. Chévez's presentation, the students divide themselves into eight groups. When Zoilita and Yolanda's group begins to discuss their activities, Zoilita proposes that the group visit two churches in their neighborhood on Sunday morning. Catholicism is very important in her community, and everyone she knows will be at mass on Sunday. The students all agree that this is a good idea and decide to make posters educating people about the rubella campaign that they can present to the church groups. Yolanda suggests that the group meet with the priest and shepherd of each church to ask for their support during the sermon. She also suggests that they invite a health expert to teach the congregation about the rubella campaign and encourage them to get vaccinated.

"Thank you for your suggestions, Zoilita and Yolanda," responds Dr. Chévez with a smile. "It is important to reach as many people as possible with correct information, and churches and community organizations are a very good way to do that."

After Dr. Chévez leaves, the children reconvene to discuss each group's ideas. One group proposes to present information about the rubella campaign during student-teacher conferences. Another group decides to accompany the people giving the vaccines to carry the coolers in which the vaccines are transported. A group of younger students decides to decorate the areas where they will administer the vaccines with posters describing the rubella vaccine and to give lemonade to the people waiting in line to receive the vaccine, which people will appreciate in the El Salvadorian heat. At the end of the meeting, each group writes a list of tasks to carry out. Completing them will contribute to the success of the rubella vaccination campaign.

During the following eight weeks, the students of Santa Sofia School work tirelessly to assist the rubella campaign in the San Miguel district. They begin working at eight every Saturday and Sunday, and don't stop until four in the afternoon. Zoilita and Yolanda's group begins by meeting with priests and shepherds to encourage them to educate their congregations about the importance of the rubella vaccination. By the end of the campaign, their efforts alone help encourage more than two thousand people to get vaccinated!

On the final Sunday of the final week of the campaign, Dr. Chévez thanks the population of San Miguel for their hard work. He gives a special thank you to the commitment of the students of Santa Sofia School for working so dedicatedly throughout the rubella campaign. "Each one of you is an excellent citizen and has demonstrated that you can participate in and successfully complete a vaccination campaign." The people of San Miguel stand on their feet and applaud the hard work of the students from Santa Sofia School.

19

DOTS

Emily Mendenhall

"DOTS" describes the role that tuberculosis (TB) has played in Ana's family. TB kills five thousand people each day, and most people who die from TB infection could survive with the provision of essential medicines because it is a treatable disease. TB is easily spread through the air when people cough, making those who live close to them more likely to get infected. Over one-third of the global population has bacteria that cause TB.

Nobody could convince Ana that there was a better place in the world than the coast. Ana smiles as she thinks about what she will do when she escapes school and has the weekend to herself. She tilts her head and closes her eyes as she envisions great blue, green, and white waves crashing against the rocks. She almost can feel the cool breeze from the Pacific Ocean bouncing off the waves and blasting through her hair. Lima has always been her home, and she can't fathom life without water.

"Ana Garcia, it is your turn! Please roll up your sleeve!" the nurse calls, bringing Ana out of her daydream and back into reality. Ana has been standing in line for her bacillus Calmette-Guérin (BCG) vaccine for two hours and is not looking forward to the needle prick.

"I'm ready; I can do this," Ana says with a weak smile as she walks forward and looks up at the nurse.

The nurse looks down at her with a tender smile. "You know, the BCG vaccine prevents many TB infections." The nurse grabs the fleshy part of her arm and sticks the needle in it before Ana can protest. "You will be lucky to prevent the tuberculosis from attacking you . . . with this outbreak and all."

Ana's blood drains from her face. She looks away from the nurse and, speedily running for the door, says, "Thanks." She doesn't look up as she passes the other students in the line waiting for their vaccine. At that instant, all she can think of is escaping the blue halls of her school and reaching the solitude she finds in one place: the ocean.

Ana lives in Carabayllo, a slum outside of Lima, Peru. She hasn't always lived in Carabayllo. Ana lived in an apartment near the center of Lima with her mother and father only two years ago. She attended a school she loved and did well there. Life wasn't easy, but she was happy.

As Ana leaves the school grounds, she picks up her pace and starts to run; she wants to escape to her mother. She is worried about her mother.

One year ago, Ana moved to Carabayllo with her mother. Her father had died suddenly from multidrug-resistant tuberculosis (MDR-TB) one year, four months, and eight days ago. She counts each day since her father's death in a calendar she keeps under the mattress she shares with her mother. It was the day everything changed. *MDR-TB*, Ana thinks to herself. She shudders a little as she repeats the acronym. *MDR-TB*. *MDR-TB is untreatable*, she mulls over again in her head. *They say that tuberculosis is treatable. I know it's treatable, but Papa's wasn't*. Ana clenches her fists and keeps moving toward her mother.

MDR-TB has become a major health problem in many countries. Bacteria have adapted, and thus the best antibiotics are no longer effective. Bacteria adapt to the environment in which they exist;

Mycobacterium tuberculosis (the bacterium that causes tuberculosis) has evolved to the point where it has become resistant to the drugs available to fight it. This resistance is most likely due to patients not completing their treatments, allowing bacteria to survive and adapt.

In the past two years, Ana and her mother have learned more than they ever had wanted to know about tuberculosis. When her father was diagnosed, they believed that he could be treated. The health center gave him dose after dose of every tuberculosis drug available. Finally, the doctor discovered that his strain of tuberculosis was resistant to every drug on the market. He died after six months of fighting the disease.

After Ana's father died, she and her mother were forced to move to the outskirts of Lima. The tuberculosis treatments had consumed all of the money they had saved. Ana's mother continues to work as a teacher, but her income is so small it is difficult to subsist on. The change that has been most difficult for Ana is living farther from the coast. The beautiful rocky coast of Lima is her favorite place to escape to. She loses herself in the energy created by the waves crashing against the rock. She often takes her journal and fleshes out her thoughts to the rhythm of the waves. Carabayllo is farther away from the coast, but she takes a bus to her favorite enclave every Saturday to regain her strength.

Ana finally reaches the door to her small home, which is built on a typical sand dune in Carabayllo. She pushes it open and smells her mother's cooking from the afternoon meal. Her mother teaches in the morning and comes home around three in the afternoon to cook and put the house in order. Ana often works in the morning as a *promotora*, educating families in Carabayllo about tuberculosis and how to prevent it. Today was one of those mornings, so she hasn't eaten since then, when her mother handed her bread and fresh cheese on the way out the door. She opens the lid to her mother's cooking and scoops out a serving of *arroz con pollo*, or chicken and rice. These days it's mostly seasoned rice only, because chicken is too expensive.

Today Ana's mother is not home when she returns from school. Six months ago Ana's mother also developed symptoms for tuberculosis.

Terrified, she went to the local health clinic, Socios en Salud, or Partners in Health, for health care. She had heard that this clinic, located near their home in Carabayllo, served tuberculosis patients. She also knew that this was a nonprofit clinic, meaning she could receive safe health care without medical bills. She wasn't able to afford more treatments and battle another bout of tuberculosis. She feared her situation would be like her husband's; she promised she would never desert Ana.

When Ana's mother visited Socios en Salud, her sputum test for tuberculosis showed that she had a treatable form of tuberculosis. Today, she cannot meet Ana at home because she is participating in DOTS. DOTS is short for "directly observed therapy, short-term." It's a proven way to fight tuberculosis—it is successful for patients with a strain of TB that can be fought by antibacterial drugs. For five months, Ana's mother has had to go to the clinic every day at six in the evening to take her medications.

Ana sits down at their table and begins to eat her rice slowly as she starts her homework. Since her mother began attending Socios en Salud, Ana has become passionate about community health. Immediately after her mother began treatment, Ana began visiting the health center and volunteering in any way she could. Only five months later, she is working with the *promotoras* in her community to educate others about tuberculosis.

As Ana flips to the final page of her book, a guide for health educators, she hears the metal door creak behind her. She quickly turns around and sees her mother walk through the door, full of life.

"Today was my last day of therapy! It is over. Tomorrow I will have another sputum test. I should now be tuberculosis-free!"

Ana jumps from the table and embraces her mother. They begin to cry and hold each other, not letting go until the other loosens her grip. Finally, Ana's mother grabs her daughter's face and says, "If only we had known of this clinic two years ago . . . ," her voice trails off, and the joy begins to seep out of her voice. She gathers her breath and says, "I am so happy to be here with you, Ana. I could not be more proud of your dedication to fighting this disease that we have battled for so long. We will make it. You and me. We will beat this disease."

Ana smiles at her mother and says, "Tomorrow, we celebrate and spend the whole day on the coast. You and me."

Ana's mother takes her daughter's hand and holds it to her face. They take in a deep breath of fresh air and know that, this time, they have won.

20

Karai Guasu's Cock-a-Doodle-Doo

Deborah Casanova

"Karai Guasu's Cock-a-Doodle-Doo" describes the important role water plays in Miguel Angel's life in Paraguay. Across the globe, women and children spend a large portion of their days collecting water, keeping them from school and other activities. Even after they have spent many hours collecting water from wells and/or nearby water sources, such as rivers and lakes, often the water is not suitable for consumption. It is difficult for many people to understand the role that water plays in the lives of people who depend on natural sources for water rather than receive it from a filtered tap. Over the course of the twenty-first century, water is projected to become one of the most important resources.

Miguel Angel often dreads the call of the rooster that serves as his family's natural alarm clock. Without fail, every morning the family's lone rooster, who Miguel Angel nicknamed Karai Guasu, or Mr. Big, lets out an energetic "cock-a-doodle-dooooooooo!" as the sun begins to poke its head up out of the calm horizon. With sleepy eyes, Miguel Angel begrudg-ingly turns from his side, rolls over onto his back, and awakens in the small dark bedroom that he shares with his two younger sisters, Lorena and Rosario.

Despite his best intentions, it takes his other natural alarm clock, his mother, Josephina, to complete the task of getting Miguel Angel out of bed! But they both know that it is 5:30 AM and there is much to be done before Miguel Angel has breakfast and leaves for school. As Miguel Angel creeps out of the bedroom, he sees the familiar sight of his mom and dad sharing maté, the hot tea drink of Paraguay. He is still too young to drink with them, but every now and then his mom will give him a sip, or a *ha*, as is said in Guarani, as he is heading out to greet the family's cows and horses.

Miguel Angel has been caring for his parent's four cows and two horses since he was six years old. Back then he was eager to prove that he could assist his father, Andres, and mother in caring for their farm. Now he often dreams of skipping his work on the farm to sleep in lon-ger, but his obligation to help his parents is too great.

At age ten, Miguel Angel is an expert at taking care of the animals. He knows the routine of each one and what they need. Miguel greets them every morning and asks them how they slept. "*Mba'e to ko, che ra'a? Mba'eicha pa pee peneko-e?*" He herds them in from the field to his house by using grunts ("Hee-yah!") and by slapping them on the backside with a small branch.

Once they near the house, he ties the cows up with worn rope because he knows that his mom will be coming out to milk them in a few minutes. These cows are extremely important to his family; they depend on them for all of their milk. Miguel Angel knows that it is criti-cal that he take good care of them, that he provide them with adequate feed and notice if they begin to look sick or moody. He knows the ani-mals well; each one has a unique personality. He often offers to help his mother with milking, because in return she may save some of the day's milk to make cheese, which he likes to eat with honey. However, usually she only makes cheese for special occasions such as a birthday or Holy

Week, the most celebrated holidays in Paraguay.

His family also depends greatly on its two new horses for transportation. Their two horses are like the wheels on a car, but in Miguel Angel's case, the car is a wooden wagon. Since his parents bought the horses, Miguel Angel has learned how to strap the horses to the wagon and "drive" by pulling on the reins. He accompanies his father to the market three hours away to sell corn and cotton during harvest season.

The horses' and Miguel Angel's greatest responsibility of the day, however, is to pull water from his family's well. The name Paraguay is a combination of the Guarani words "*pará*," meaning "ocean," "*gua*," meaning "from," and "*y*," which means "water"; read together, the parts yield "water that goes to the water." However, not all Paraguayans have a dependable source of water to drink and use for daily living. Miguel Angel and his family live in the north of Paraguay, in San Pedro, where water is in limited supply. They draw their water from very deep wells every day.

The wells in Miguel Angel's neighborhood are some of the deepest in San Pedro—most go at least fifty meters into the ground, which is the length of half of a football field! Before his parents bought the horses, Miguel Angel's mom and sisters would tie a bucket onto a rope and lower it fifty meters down into the water below. Then, working as a tag team, one of them would pull the bucket up by grabbing the top of the rope and handing it to another one, who would pull it further downward. One of his sisters would then walk the full bucket to the house, carefully balancing it on her head, and pour it into a big metal *tambor*, a bin originally used to hold grains.

It took them at least two hours a day, every day, to fill up the tambor with the water they needed to take baths, cook, clean dishes, water their garden, and, of course, drink. Water is also needed for making *tereré*, the cold version of maté. Laundry, which Miguel Angel's mom and sisters do by hand, requires even more buckets of water.

There have been times when there just hasn't been enough water in the well for everything. Last year, Miguel's mom had to stop watering their garden because there wasn't enough water to spare; the vegetables and herbs withered, dried up, and died. Miguel Angel's mother and sisters had to walk two miles to the nearest stream to bring back buckets of water for drinking, cooking, and bathing.

At times the water in the well is so shallow that it gets muddy. Miguel's mom strains the water through a thin cloth and pours it into a *kambushi*, a clay storage pot for water that cools it for drinking. She also adds a few drops of liquid chlorine bleach to purify the water and make it safer for Miguel Angel and his sisters to drink.

Even so, Miguel Angel and his sisters have been sick many times with tummy aches. His teachers and community health worker say that *bichos*, or parasites, come from the unclean water, set up residence in his stomach, and make it ache and swell and gurgle inside. With his mother and sisters, Miguel Angel has made the two-hour trip to see the nurse at the local clinic for medicine. Even with the medicine, Miguel and his sisters still get sick from time to time. Miguel often feels so sick that he can't pay attention at school or play with his friends.

Miguel Angel's family dreams of having clean running water in their house and even of having a flush toilet someday, just like the kind they have seen in his cousin's house in the nearby town of Santani. Some nearby neighborhoods, with the help of local engineers, have begun to build their own water pumps and storage tanks using their own materials and their own funds as well as grants from various nonprofit organizations. With just the flip of a switch, the water is pumped from the deep well into a storage tank above and then out to the pipes and faucets. It will be a while, though, before Miguel Angel's family has enough money saved for such a project—the priority for now is buying food and paying school fees.

On this early morning, the horses are a blessing. Miguel Angel ties one end of the rope to the bucket and drops the bucket into the well. He ties the other end of the rope to the horse's harness and leads the horse across the yard to pull the full bucket back up from the well. Miguel Angel and his horse pull the water much more quickly than Miguel Angel's mother and sisters could pull it by hand. Once he is back at the house, he unties the bucket from the horse's harness and brings it inside for his mother.

After chores, Josephina makes him *cocido*, a morning drink made with tea herbs, water, and sugar caramelized with a piece of charcoal, and gives him hardened bread rolls to eat. Miguel Angel loves dipping the rolls until they are soft and dripping with warm *cocido* . . . mmmn!

This is Miguel Angel's favorite time of day because he sits with his mother and sisters and talks about school and reads stories aloud at the breakfast table. Even though his mother is busy preparing for the day, she always spends a few moments with her children before they must bathe and get ready for school. After Miguel Angel has finished breakfast and cooled off from the morning's activity, he rushes off to clean himself up and get dressed for school. He then steps out of the house for the second time that morning, breathing in deeply as he walks with his sisters to the neighborhood schoolhouse.

21

Rosa's Farm

Emily Mendenhall

"Rosa's Farm" describes life on a Mapuche reservation in southern Chile. The relocation of the Mapuche people to the reservations has greatly influenced their health, culture, and lifestyle. Even though families have grown, the Mapuche people have not been granted access to more land, which has meant that newer generations have not been able to stay in their rural communities but have been compelled to move to urban areas. The narrative also describes the importance of intergenerational relationships and activism.

"Wake up, *mija!*" Mama shouts from the kitchen. Rosa slowly opens her eyes and deeply inhales the aroma of her mother's freshly baked bread. The smell of bread is mixed with the smell of wood burning, the sound of roosters crowing, and the bite of the cold spring air. Rosa rolls over onto one side and pulls her quilt tightly beneath her chin. Rosa knows that it's best to stay in bed on October mornings because when she moves, she loses the heat hidden under her blankets.

"Rosa, wake up, it's time for school!" her Mama shouts from the kitchen door. The kitchen is detached from the rest of the house, so Rosa knows she has a few more minutes in bed before her mother reaches her room. The kitchen is lined with wood for the fire pit, where the bread bakes slowly. There is a hole in the ceiling of the kitchen so the smoke can escape—sometimes the smoke makes Mama cough a lot. Rosa loves making bread by covering the fresh dough under hot coals in the fire pit. However, this morning Rosa doesn't wake up in time to help make the morning bread.

Still under the covers, Rosa smiles when her mother enters her room with warm tea and fresh bread. Rosa dips her bread in her tea to make it nice and soft before she eats it. After breakfast and a lecture from her mother, Rosa gets out of bed to dress. Mama helps her put on her school uniform, home-sewn navy pants and a light blue sweater. All students in Rosa's school live in the same neighborhood and wear the same uniform, and they can all walk to school in under fifteen minutes.

Rosa knows everyone in Trompulo, her *comunidad*, or community. Families rarely move off their land, and Rosa knows everyone by name. Rosa's parents built the house she lives in when they were married, and her *abuelita* (grandmother) lives only steps away. Rosa's *abuelita* has lived on the same land since Rosa's birth, and Rosa can't think of ever living far from her family.

Having dressed and eaten, Rosa prepares to walk to school with her older brother, Roberto. "Don't forget your jacket, Rosa, it's chilly outside," says Roberto on his way out the door. Rosa looks up at him and smiles—Roberto wakes up before the sun rises to do his chores and has already been outside for an hour. He collects water from the pump in the backyard so Mama can make the bread for the family. Every morning for three years, Roberto has fed the chickens and milked the goats before breakfast. Almost everyone in Trompulo drinks goat milk. When she returns home from school, Rosa mixes her goat milk with sugar and drinks it in two big gulps!

"Roberto, do you think Mama and Papa learned the same things in school as we do now?" Rosa asks her brother as she runs to catch up with him. Their school is a tiny building with two rooms, covered with chipped white paint and a green stripe around the walls. One room is for the younger students and the other is for the older students. Rosa recently began studying with the older students, so she and Roberto are now in the same classroom. "I'm sure they learned some of the same things, Rosa. But times change, and you never know what's going to happen next. Just think about the stories *abuelita* tells us about where the *comunidad* used to be. You never know how things will turn out."

Rosa's *abuelita* loves storytelling, and Rosa loves to hear stories about the Mapuche people. Rosa is extremely curious about her history and spends hours upon hours listening to *abuelita*'s stories about the past. Mapuche means "people of the land" in Mapudungun, *abuelita*'s language. Rosa is proud of these stories because, although the past has been one of struggle, it has also been one that shows the unity of the Mapuche people, and she knows that she is a part of her community's future.

"Roberto, tell me again about Abuelita—about how different it was when she was a girl like me," Rosa asks her wise brother. Roberto turns to his sister and knowingly begins, "Rosa, Mapuche have always been farmers. We have farmed the same region for hundreds of years, before there were any airplanes or cars or radios. When Abuelita was a girl, their farm was miles away from here, and the family moved here when Mother was a young girl—you know that!"

"Oh, Roberto, I know, but will you tell me about the history of the Mapuche?" Rosa is ten and has only begun learning Mapudungun in school. She loves the many stories her *abuelita* has told her, and she already knows many words in her *abuelita*'s language. As Rosa has begun learning Mapudungun, she has become curious about the history of the words.

"OK, but this is the last time," Roberto says, grinning, to Rosa, knowing that it will not be the last. "As long as the rains come and as long as we have land to grow food, we will never be hungry. We have been farmers for centuries—the Mapuche lived here before any Spaniards came to the Americas; we were here before Christopher Columbus. We are strong people with a rich history but have suffered because people have tried to take over our land for many years. We have fought to keep our land, but now we must fight to keep our culture alive as well. As many of our friends move away to big cities, they are separated from their families and their traditions change. For example, if we lived in the city, Mama would likely buy bread at the market rather than bake it each morning at home. People often depend less on the land in cities. Trompulo is a rural *comunidad*, and we depend on the land."

Trompulo is a village of fifty families, and every family is Mapuche. The total population is less than three hundred people, most of whom are farmers. Rosa's parents farm, and they rely on the wheat they produce to feed their family. They also grow fruits, vegetables, and herbs in the garden. They visit the grocery store to buy tea and coffee once every month, but they grow most of their food at home. During the spring and summer when there is more rain, Rosa's family sells wheat at the market. Rosa's family members are subsistence farmers, which means that rather than buying their food from other farmers or stores, they themselves grow all the food they need to survive.

Rosa often helps her mother collect food from the greenhouse where they grow their vegetables. They grow tomatoes, carrots, peppers, and many herbs. Rosa's favorite herb is cilantro; she helps her mother prepare for supper by cutting the herbs. She also likes to collect the chili peppers, but she has to be very careful because they make her hands burn if she touches the seeds. They also have an apple tree that produces the reddest apples in all of Trompulo.

As Rosa and Roberto reach the road, they see María running up the path toward them. "María!" Rosa squeals. María is Rosa's best friend. Her family has apple trees too. María lives across the road from Rosa, but Maria's walk to the road takes ten minutes because she has to cross acres of farmland on foot. María loves the walk through the farm and the smell of the wheat as the wind blows. María pulls her coat collar up to her ears to protect them from the cold. She finally meets Roberto and Rosa at the gate of her house, and together they all continue their walk to school.

"*Buenos días*, María!" Rosa and Roberto sing together. All of Rosa's friends live on farms in Trompulo, but there are a few other professions besides farming where she lives. María's mother is a healer: she doctors, counsels, and supports her patients spiritually by talking with them about God and the traditional cosmology of their ancestors. María's mother usually visits sick people in their homes, just like Mapuche healers did in the past. María's mother is the only healer in Trompulo, and many people depend on her guidance.

"Roberto, will you miss our walks to school next year? I can't believe you plan to leave us for Temuco!" María says. Roberto nudges María in jest. Trompulo's school only offers six grades. After six years, students either travel to Temuco to attend school, begin working on the farm, or begin another trade. "You're right, María, it will be a big change for Rosa and me—she might not ever make it to school!" jokes Roberto. Rosa sticks her tongue out at Roberto and looks down at the ground. "You know that I'll visit you next year, *hermana*," says Roberto. "I have the opportunity to continue with school, so Mom and Dad say that I must. Besides, I get to live with our *tío* in Temuco!"

"Roberto, why can't you stay at home to help Papa with the farm next year?" Rosa asks as they turn the corner with the school in sight. "Oh, Rosa, you know that I can't stay and make a living on the farm. There is not enough land for both of us to farm, and I can't depend on it for my future." Rosa knows this is true, but she is upset that her brother plans to leave her next year. "Besides, if I continue with my studies and do well enough to attend the university, I can really help our family and our people." Roberto becomes lost in his thoughts. And then he says, "I will become a lawyer and protect Mapuche lands and defend our rights as Mapuche people. I know I can make a difference."

Rosa smiles as she hears her brother's speech about his future. Even though he is still young, he is already very driven, and she's proud of him. *It's true that things are different now*, Rosa thinks. Her *abuelita* tells stories of days that are gone forever, days when everyone could farm. Then there was enough farmland for children to live near their parents and grandparents after they grew up and had families of their own. But now land is restricted. Roberto is right: the Mapuche have little political power in the government to make sure that their land is protected. Today, they fear losing not only their land but also their identity that is woven into the land.

"Roberto, I wish there was enough land for us to share so our families could be neighbors, just like we live next door to Abuelita!" Rosa said to her brother. After moving to Temuco for school, many young people often stay to raise their families, because there is more work opportunity in the city. Some of Roberto's friends will move to Santiago—the capital of Chile—seeking even more opportunity. Today more than half of all Mapuche living in Chile live in Santiago.

"Come on Rosa, we are going to be late for school!" Roberto calls over his shoulder.

Rosa stops ten feet from the schoolhouse gate and pronounces proudly, "At least you will come back for the summer fiesta—everyone comes back in December!" Rosa grins as she thinks about this most important holiday, which is celebrated on December 21st. It is the most anticipated time of year, because the whole town comes together for a big feast. No one wants to miss this celebration, because there is plenty of food, music, and stories; family members return to Trompulo from Temuco, and even Santiago. Rosa also knows that wherever they move, Abuelita's stories will remain a part of them.

After opening the gate and trudging halfway to the schoolhouse, Roberto returns to grab Rosa and Maria's hands and huff, "Rosa . . . María, we are going to be late for school. You will never make it next year without me!" The girls look at each other and laugh as they walk over the threshold of the schoolhouse with seconds to spare.

MALI

SENEGAL   BURKINA   GHANA
           FASO

TANZANIA

ZAMBIA

SOUTH
AFRICA

Part 5

AFRICA

22

The Pen Pals

Sarah Raskin

"The Pen Pals" is about the e-mail–based relationship between Sibonelo, a young man in South Africa, and Joy, a young woman in the United States. Although they live in different countries, they are both struggling with gender-based violence: Thabisa, who is Sibonelo's sister, and Joy are being abused by their boyfriends. This narrative aims to increase awareness of gender-based violence and show that there is a way out.

Sibonelo Mfeka is a sixteen-year-old boy from the Kennedy Road settlements in Durban, South Africa. Joy Proffit is a fifteen-year-old girl from Pulaski, a small town in southwestern Virginia. Sibonelo and Joy have been corresponding for six years, since they were matched during a primary school pen pal exchange. Their friendship began when they sent each other letters in class packets. However, since Sibonelo started working as an assistant at the local internet café two years ago, they now mostly use e-mail. Although in their early correspondence Sibonelo and Joy discussed their likes and dislikes, their daily lives, their aspirations, and current events, their e-mails have recently turned to a more personal topic: the bullying, abuse, and control that they are each experiencing.

Dear Sibonelo,

THANKS A LOT 4 sending me a birthday e-card! It's sooooo sweet of U 2 remember even if it's easy 4 U since yr sister and I share that day so maybe I'll say "Thanks a little" instead of "Thanks a lot," so U don't get too full of yrself ;) How is Thabisa BTW?

Sibonelo stood up quickly. He sucked his breath over his teeth, cooling them as he always did when he was nervous. *How do I answer that question*, Sibonelo thought, *when I'm so unsure of the answer myself?* He decided to keep reading Joy's e-mail, so he sat down and leaned closer to the monitor.

Sometimes I'm jealous that yr so close with her. Ever since she got her driver's license my sister doesn't really want anything to do with me. But that's OK coz Greg has his license and a nice new truck so I don't need her anyway LOL. Yup, Greg's still in the picture can U believe it????

Howz yr love life? I'm sure U meet lots of cute girls working at the internet café but IMHO U should only keep that job if U can do it after school. It's not worth giving up yr education, even if U have to wait to earn money 4 yr family. Just a few more years till U finish secondary school and then U can go be Donald Trump LOL. Knowing U, Nelson Mandela is more like it. How R U celebrating Human Rights Day?

I have to get back to my homework so I can call Greg right at 8 like he likes. Last time I forgot to he got really mad and accused me of cheating on him WHICH I'M NOT!!! Anyway, I'm wishing

U a very happy day and a good night's sleep.
With hugs from yr friend,
Joy

PS: Happy anniversary of our friendship. Can U believe we've been writing for six WHOLE YEARS????

Six years, thought Sibonelo, marveling at how close Joy and he felt to each other, even though they had never met. They knew as much about each other as best friends could possibly know, and sometimes they thought it was fate that had brought them together. They both loved basketball, Maroon 5, and barbeques (*braai*, Sibonelo taught Joy to call them). They both preferred geography to other subjects, and they dreamed of visiting the other's country. Also, both Joy's and Sibonelo's fathers were killed in 2005: Joy's father was a soldier in Iraq and Sibonelo's was an activist who protested against the government for failing to provide essential services like water and electricity to their settlement. (*We have settlements too*, Joy had written to Sibonelo, solemnly, for the first time really understanding his poverty. *We call them "slums."*)

And now, thought Sibonelo, *I fear that we share* this. Sibonelo had been increasingly concerned about Joy's relationship with her boyfriend Greg, just as he was concerned about the way that his sister's boyfriend, Bhekani, treated her.

Dear Joy, Sibonelo started to write in reply . . .

"Sibbo!?!" Bhekani interrupted, his voice bellowing into the internet café and his big feet showing off his clean, new Air Jordans. Sibonelo moved the mouse to another window, a spreadsheet. In just two short years, Sibonelo had risen from sweeping up the café and fetching supplies to helping Bhekani manage his various internet cafés. He had even set up accounting software and a membership system. Sibonelo was proud that he was working hard and contributing to the household income, although he hated working for his sister's boyfriend. He hoped one day he could open his own chain of internet cafés and rid his family of this man completely.

"Sibbo!" Bhekani repeated, "Howzit, little man? Good business this afternoon?"

"It's alright" replied Sibonelo. "About two-thirds full. A couple of first-timers."

"Kwaai, bro, good," Bhekani interrupted. "Keep bringing in those Benjies. I have to meet Amala." Sibonelo paused and looked Bhekani in the eye with as much courage as he could. Bhekani stared him down. "Look, little man. The girls love a man with ambition. *Monna ke thaka, o naba.* A man's gotta spread the love around. Now don't squeal 'cause there's nothing to tell your sister. Thabisa's still my main woman. I just like to keep some sweet things on reserve."

Bhekani bumped Sibonelo aside to log into his e-mail. Sibonelo's face reddened as he realized he forgot to log out of his own account. "Ahhh, Sibbo," Bhekani said slyly, staring at the e-mail from Joy, "you understand. I'm sure you're not tellin' the girls around here that your heart really belongs to an American." Bhekani slapped Sibonelo on the back, laughing. "Good job, son. Soon you'll be as good as me!" His tone changed. "But I mean it. If you want to keep your job, don't tell your sister anything. ANYTHING. Or I won't think twice about putting you in your place after I get done with her."

Bhekani slammed the door behind him, leaving Sibonelo to run the internet café alone until it closed at midnight. Sibonelo sighed. It was becoming harder and harder to do his homework that late, when he had to be up by 5:30 AM to do the three-bus commute to Ohlange High School. And yet, he had to maintain good grades to keep his scholarship. *Joy is right,* Sibonelo thought, *I really need to finish secondary school and, hopefully, with luck, I can go to a university.* But for now he had a more urgent problem: how to handle the way Bhekani tried to control Thabisa. He sighed.

Dear Joy, Sibonelo wrote early the next morning from the computer lab at school,

Howzit with U? I'm OK. Tired.

I am trying to take yr advice and keep my focus on school but it's hard. Last night I worked til midnite to cover for Bhekani. He was already there when I got home from work, eating the plate of dinner that Mama made for me. He stared me in the eyes until I had to look away, and when I did I noticed a bruise on Thabisa's thigh. I wonder if he did that to her. She doesn't think I hear him scolding her late at night, calling her names and telling her that she's worthless. But I do. I can't concentrate on my homework when Bhekani shouts like that.

Sibonelo paused. He reread his words in disbelief. It seemed that the values of respecting others and treating everyone equally that his father had inculcated in his family had died with him. Before, Sibonelo's parents never would have accepted a man who mistreated Thabisa into their family. But now Bhekani considered himself the man of the house, entitled to do whatever he wanted, and Sibonelo's sister and mother accepted that. Sibonelo sighed. He worried that Joy's family was experiencing something similar. Her father would never have let her go on dates with boys who were old enough to drive, but with her mom still in shock over her father's death, there were fewer rules in Joy's house. Sibonelo continued typing.

This year I am taking Thabisa with me on Human Rights Day. We will celebrate at a festival in Pietermaritzburg on the University of KwaZulu-Natal campus. Did U know that's where Gandhi got his start as an activist? It's true! Cross yr fingers that I will meet a university official who will offer me a scholarship LOL. No, really, cross yr fingers that I will be able to introduce Thabisa to others who are kind and who give her sihlohipha. Respect. I must show Thabisa that Bhekani's abuse violates her human rights and convince her to break up with him. Of course, I will have to quit my job but I am prepared to make that sacrifice. I can find other work.

*I'm sorry 2 B so serious in this e-mail but I know U can
handle it. I have a lot on my mind. Can U IM soon? Is it spring
yet, and warm? Did U listen to that Zola link I sent U? He will
perform at Human Rights Day and I will request a song for U!*

A hug from yr friend,

Sibonelo

Over three weeks had gone by since Sibonelo had heard from Joy. It was
unusual for her to take so long to reply. Sibonelo decided to write to her
again as soon as he got to school.

Dear Joy,

R U OK? I miss hearing from U. I hope that U R fine.

*How R things with U? Things R OK here. Thabisa and I had
an OK time at the Human Rights Day festival. Unfortunately,
Bhekani came with us. He spent almost the whole time drinking
beer, flirting with other girls, and criticizing the speakers who
encouraged women to become empowered and do things like own
their own businesses, fight for their rights, and leave abusive relationships. But it was fine because I think that Thabisa has started
to see Bhekani's true colors. She spoke with some social workers
who run a shelter and a hotline for women who suffer from abuse. I
saw her put their phone number on a small piece of paper and tuck
it in her shoe when Bhekani wasn't looking. I will try to support
her by telling Bhekani that I can't work so many hours during final
exams, so that he will be occupied with work and she will have the
freedom to call the abuse hotline. And I will try to have patience
with her if she doesn't leave him as quickly as I hope she will.*

*My school project on the rivers of North America is going
really well. Thank U for those photos of the New River! My teacher
will be very impressed that I have photos of one of the oldest rivers
in the world, taken by someone who lives right near it!*

Joy, I miss U. Please write back when U can.
With a big hug from yr friend,
Sibonelo

At the end of the day Sibonelo was pleasantly surprised to find an e-mail awaiting him. The subject line said "from Joy," but he did not recognize the return address.

Dear Sibonelo,

Hiiiiiiiiiiiiiiiiiiiiiii! I'm SO SORRY to take so long to write U back. I had to sign up 4 a new e-mail address, so I needed my mom's permission to get one. Long story short, Greg got into my old e-mail account and he read all of my e-mails! He was SO MAD at me for how frequently we write. He accused me of being in love with U and just using him for rides and stuff. I tried to explain that U R my best friend, that U R like a brother not a boyfriend but he wouldn't listen.

So I had 2 chill out on writing U and convince him that I really love him and that I mean it. He said Oh yeah, prove it, and so I did. I proved it even though I was scared and I'm not allowed to have him in my room with the door closed. But then my mom got home from work and walked in on us and everyone was mad at me. Greg apologized to Mom and she believed him, but then behind her back he grabbed my arm and squeezed really really hard and told me that if she tried to put him in jail for having relations with a minor, he'd get us all, even my sister 2.

I dunno Sibonelo. I know he loves me and he's just jealous of our friendship because he knows that no other guy can love me as much as he does, but sometimes I get scared of him and other times I feel ashamed because I let him treat me badly and I accept his apology even when I think he doesn't mean it and other times I let him do stuff that I'm not really comfortable doing because I want to show him how much I love him. He's really the first guy to tell me he loves me.

I wish U were here so U could be the good brother to me that U are to Thabisa. That's why my mom gave me a new e-mail account to keep writing to U, in secret from Greg. She says that U R a good influence and that U R smart and caring in the way that a man SHOULD be. What do U think I should do?

A great big hug from,

Joy

Sibonelo sat back in his chair, cooling his teeth with his breath. What could he say to Joy to convince her that Greg's so-called love was really abuse and that it would only get worse as time went on? He was already having a hard time convincing Thabisa of this fact, and he lived with her! Sibonelo decided that he needed some help figuring out what advice to give Joy. But first, he had to get away from his own bully.

"Bhekani!" Sibonelo shouted in the doorway of the internet café, his voice breathless and raspy from running all the way from the bus stop. "BHEKANI!"

"Whaddup, little bro?" Bhekani shouted back, as Sibonelo ran in the door. "You on fire or something?"

"Almost," Sibonelo replied. "Almost, man. I'm sorry but I can't cover for you today at work. I need to go home and sort some things out with Mama," he said, cringing at the white lie he was about to tell. "She called the principal today to talk with him about my study habits even after I asked her not to. You know, man," he continued, knowing how to get Bhekani to agree with him, "it's a man's job to take care of himself. I don't need my mother making me look stupid and immature by handling my business."

"Hehehe, yeah, you're right Sibonelo," Bhekani said, calling him by his full name for the first time. "You go handle your business. Your mother's gotta learn not to get in the way of her little man! But you'd better plan to leave school early tomorrow so you can make up these hours you'll owe me."

"Yessir," Sibonelo replied, and ran back out the door.

❧

Dear Joy, he began his e-mail later that night at the internet café nearer to his home, where he hoped to get a job soon.

I have read yr e-mail a few times, and I am very concerned about U. I understand that there will be times in our lives when we won't be able to write as frequently as we have in the past. Nevertheless, I am worried about the reason why U didn't write.

Please forgive my directness, but I need to say this: control is not love. If U think that Greg demonstrates his love for U by making yr decisions for U, by forcing U to do things, by threatening U, and by being physically violent toward U, I have to correct U. That is wrong. I understand how much it means to U that he says he loves U. Perhaps he really does. But if he does love U, he will find a way to manage his anger before he treats U even worse.

I hope that U don't mind, but after I read yr e-mail I asked Thabisa for her advice, as a woman who also has a controlling boyfriend. Thabisa calls the abused women's hotline when she can, and she has been to a women's group at the community center twice. I asked her, "What convinced U to try to make a change in yr life and yr relationship?" She said, "U. U held up a mirror to me. That day at the Human Rights Day festival, U showed me that there are better ways women can be treated than how Bhekani treats me. U introduced me to the women from the hotline, but even more important, U and yr friends demonstrated to me how good men treat women with sihlohipha. *I watched U speak with girls that day, Sibonelo, and U really lived up to the meaning of yr name. U were an Example. I decided then that I wanted a boyfriend who is as good to me as my little brother, who I'm so proud of, is to the girls he is interested in."*

Thabisa's compliment means a lot to me, but even more important is that she is trying to take care of herself. She helped me find out that there's a hotline for girls in America who have controlling boyfriends, too. It is called Love is Respect, and U can chat with someone online or call the hotline at 1–866–331–9474. I hope U call this number and talk with someone. But I won't be upset if U don't. U are my best friend and I will be patient with U, but I hope that U decide that finding some help and maybe taking a break from Greg is a good idea.

The wise women of South Africa say "Wa thinth' abafazi, wa thinth' imbokoto," which means "If U strike a woman, U strike our foundation." This is true in yr society too. Men who are bad to women are hurting not only the women but also their community and their country. U R right, Joy, Nelson Mandela is much more of a role model for me than Donald Trump. I hope that U join me in the struggle for justice, Joy, starting with yr own. U R a precious gem and U deserve yr human rights.

With the biggest hug I've ever sent,
Sibonelo

Walking back to his home, Sibonelo passed the homes of his neighbors. From some of them, he heard children playing and mothers singing. From others, he heard silence. And from others still, he heard men shouting at women, the sounds of slaps and children crying and dogs growling.

We have so much work to do, Sibonelo thought to himself as he reached his home. *But I'm prepared to do it.* He sat down with his school assignment and worked late into the night with a renewed energy.

23

Innocence's Journey

Verna Miller Case

"Innocence's Journey" explores a young boy's quest to care for his mother as she suffers with AIDS. They live in Zambia, where the prevalence of HIV/ AIDS is approximately 19–26 percent in urban areas and 9–12 percent in rural areas. Innocence's mother has little access to medical care. In many rural villages around the world, health clinics are far away and difficult to reach due to lack of transportation, and some people have to walk days to reach a health post supported by a trained nurse or technician.

The rooster crowed twice, and Innocence rolled onto his back on his sleeping mat. He stared up at the thatched roof of his home. It was still dark outside, but the full moon provided enough light for him to see his mother's cooking utensils wedged in the grass bundles of the roof above him. Innocence listened to his mother's labored breathing and knew that it was time for him to get moving, but the winter morning was cold, and he didn't want to give up the warmth of his blanket.

Innocence was due in school in three hours, but he would not be going to school today. As was the custom for the eldest son, he would get help for his mother. Her coughing had worsened over the past few months. Although his mother was treated by a traditional healer who had comforted her with concoctions of herbs and root teas, the medicine was now gone. Innocence thought about the rural health center he had heard about from other children at school, but he worried that his mother was too sick and too weak to travel that far by foot.

Innocence formulated a plan. He would find the doctor who worked at Mwandi Hospital, and he would ask him for medicine to help his mother. Innocence met the doctor last September when he and his schoolmates traveled to the large village of Mwandi for a track and field event that involved children from primary schools throughout the Western Province of Zambia.

Innocence was the star soccer player at his primary school. On that early morning last September, he and his teammates were ahead by one goal in the championship game with only minutes left to play. Innocence was the team's fastest striker. He had the ball and headed for the goal. As he ran toward the goal, the defender on the other team tackled him from the side. Innocence's legs flew into the air, and when he hit the ground he heard his arm snap. Trying hard not to cry, he rolled in the sandy soil holding his injured arm close to his body.

Innocence remembered being swept up in the arms of a very large man with a kind face. Without saying a word, the man carried him off the field. Innocence looked into the man's eyes and fought back his tears. The man said, "You're a tough little guy, aren't you? We'll take care of your arm. I hope your teammates can hold the lead without you."

Innocence later learned the benevolent man was the doctor at Mwandi Hospital. After arriving at the hospital, the doctor placed Innocence on a table in a room just inside the hospital's main entrance.

With an amazingly gentle touch, the doctor examined Innocence's arm. As he worked, the doctor talked about his young son, who he hoped would grow up to be as fast and strong as Innocence. Innocence wanted to show the doctor exactly how strong he was, but the pain was terrible. He cried out as the doctor, with the help of a nurse, pulled his arm until the bones snapped back in place. "Sorry," the doctor said. "You are very brave." Innocence felt his lips trembling, and he blinked hard to keep the tears from welling over his eyelids. Then the doctor smiled and rubbed the top of Innocence's head. "The nurse will put your arm in a splint, and then you can go back to the field. You can celebrate your victory with your teammates."

But after his arm was in the splint, Innocence did not go back to the playing fields. He followed the doctor as he made his rounds in the hospital. He stood in the hall as the doctor went into the children's ward. He listened to the doctor's soft, reassuring voice. Innocence knew the children were terminally sick, but some of them even laughed at the doctor's jokes. He was mesmerized by the hospital, its equipment, and the differences between this doctor's medicine and the medicine used by the healer.

For the rest of that day, Innocence followed the doctor as he moved from ward to ward, as he talked with nurses, and as he examined newborn babies. In the middle of the afternoon, the doctor asked Innocence to sit with him on a bench in the hall. At first they sat there quietly, then the big man spoke, "Well, you seem to be quite curious about my work."

Innocence said, "You are very different from the healer in my village."

"Yes, I think that is true," said the doctor, "but both of us want to help people."

"Thank you for fixing my arm. You are a very good healer. I would like to be a healer like you some day."

The doctor smiled. "Perhaps you will. Right now though, I think you should join your team back at the field. I understand they need your help to carry the championship trophy home."

Innocence got up from the bench and walked to the hospital door. When he turned to say good-bye, the doctor was already gone.

Ever since that September day, Innocence dreamed of becoming a doctor. But he was not sure if his dreams would become reality. His father had moved to Lusaka, the capital of Zambia, a year ago and had not returned to the village. Innocence was the head of the house now and was responsible for his four brothers and sisters. It was unlikely that he would be able to attend secondary school and so becoming a doctor would never be possible.

Innocence rolled off of his sleeping mat and rose to his feet. He glanced at his brothers and sisters and then went to his mother's bed. She opened her eyes and smiled at him. "I'm going to start the fire, Momma," he said. "Then I'll get the others ready for school." She kissed his bent head, and he gave her a hug. She looked so thankful and desperate at the same time. Unable to watch her sad eyes any longer, he turned and grabbed his jacket from the pile of clothes on the floor beside the door.

The air outside the mud hut was crisp, and Innocence could see his breath as he grabbed firewood. Within minutes his skilled hands had the fire blazing. His sisters and brothers began to come out of the hut. On cold mornings, they tried to warm up as much as possible by the fire before beginning the walk to school.

Innocence prepared the lunches for his brothers and sisters. The main diet of the Lozi people, his tribe, was *nshima*. Innocence spooned this cornmeal mash into enamelware pots for each of them. They carried these pots to school, and at lunch they ate the *nshima* by scooping it out of the pots with their fingers. His brothers and sisters did not notice that he prepared an unusually large pot for himself that morning. When the pots were full, they called good-bye to their mother and headed down the sandy road that led through the center of the village.

Most of the village was awake by the time they began their trek. Other children joined their procession as they walked along. Friends met and greeted one another in their native language of Silozi. There was much giggling as the boys teased the girls and then tumbled down the road doing cartwheels to show off. As they were leaving the village, the sun was peeking over the horizon. Innocence glanced back and looked at the cluster of eight thatched-roofed homes that made up his small village.

The barefooted children walked along the main road for about eight kilometers and turned on to a side road that led to their school. Innocence stayed at the back of the group and whispered his plans to his brother. Slowing his pace, Innocence watched the other children disappear behind a bend in the road. When they were completely out of sight, he turned back to the main road.

With the sun now warming his back, Innocence ran or walked for the next several hours. The loose sand on the road caused him to tire quickly. He passed the healer's herd of cattle and recognized two of the cows that his mother had given to the healer in payment for her treatments. Innocence hoped that the hospital would allow him to pay for his mother's medicine by doing odd jobs. He had no other way to pay. He decided to take his mind off of his worries by practicing his multiplication tables. Being good at math, he knew, was important if you wanted to be a doctor. Perhaps his dream might come true, if he tried hard enough.

Around noon, Innocence stopped to rest under the shade of a tree. Although Innocence's bare feet were calloused and tough, he still felt the heat rising from the sandy soil. He decided to eat his lunch. He began scooping his *nshima* with his fingers and was distracted by an eagle flying overhead. Innocence lionized eagles. They were powerful birds, and he loved to watch them soar over the bush. Right now, Innocence wished that he was an eagle flying to the hospital.

Innocence finished his *nshima* quickly and began his journey once again. He reached a small village in about an hour. He found the water pump in the center of the village and began pumping. He drank and then splashed the water over his body. A woman walking toward the pump started yelling because he was wasting the precious water. He knew that what she said was true, but the water felt so refreshing that he hated to stop. Sheepishly, he looked up at the woman and apologized. He told her about his mother and about his journey to the hospital to get medicine for her.

The woman asked him if he would like some food. He thanked her but said that he needed to keep going if he was going to reach the hospital by nightfall. She shook her head in disbelief. "My son, you will never get there before dark. You will need to run half of the night to get to the hospital. You should go to the rural health center; it is only a few kilometers from here."

"But I need to see the doctor," Innocence said. "He is the one who will help me."

"Maybe the nurse at the center can contact the doctor for you." Innocence thought for a moment. Perhaps the woman was right. He decided that he would go to the center to see if the nurse could help him.

Innocence reached the center by midafternoon. As he approached he saw a Land Rover driving away from the front of the center. Innocence guessed that it must be a hospital vehicle. His heart started racing, and he started sprinting toward the car. Maybe the driver would take him to the hospital to see the doctor. Innocence yelled as loud as he could, but the vehicle moved faster, the dust filling the air in its wake. He ran harder, his arms reaching out ahead of him as if trying to grab the Land Rover and pull it back.

Innocence did not see the stake sticking out of the ground. When his leg hit the stake, it created a huge gash down the length of his shin. He fell and rolled to his side, clutching his bleeding leg with his hands. He sobbed in despair. He had failed. He would never get to the hospital, and his mother would not get the help she needed.

The center's nurse heard Innocence's cries and came out of the mud-walled building. When she saw Innocence, she ran to him. The bleeding was heavy and the wound needed stitches, but he would be fine.

She helped Innocence to his feet and put his arm around her shoulder. When they got inside, the nurse said, "It's too bad that the doctor just left; he would have stitched you up and gotten you back on your feet in no time! Now, let's look at this cut."

The nurse glanced up as Innocence's face started to quiver. Innocence shook his head with disappointment—he was so close to his goal without realizing it. Now he would not see the doctor or get to the hospital. The tears began again, and he could not stop crying.

The nurse mistook Innocence's reaction for fear and said, "Don't worry. I will numb the wound before I begin."

As the nurse put the first stitch in Innocence's leg, they heard the sound of a vehicle approaching. Both Innocence and the nurse looked through the door when the Land Rover stopped in front of the center. Innocence was afraid to hope that the doctor had returned. He watched the door of the Land Rover open. There was no mistaking that the big man who stepped down from the car was the doctor he had spent so long trying to meet again.

When the doctor walked through the door of the center, he recognized Innocence. "Well, if it isn't my football star. What's this, injured again?" Then he looked at the nurse. "I forgot my stethoscope." He smiled, picked up the stethoscope, and turned toward the door.

The words just blurted out of Innocence's mouth. "My momma needs you."

The doctor turned, looked into Innocence's teary eyes, and said, "Tell me about your mother, and I'll finish stitching that leg of yours."

By the time the doctor finished his job, Innocence had finished telling his story. "Now let's go see your mum and see about the medicine she needs," said the doctor.

Riding in the doctor's Land Rover was a treat for Innocence. He had never been in a car before, and it certainly wasn't like riding in an oxcart! The doctor asked Innocence a lot of questions about school. Innocence wanted the doctor to like him, so he tried to sound very smart. When they were close to his village, Innocence decided to ask the doctor a question—a question that he feared to have answered.

"Is my mother going to die?"

The doctor turned and looked into Innocence's solemn eyes. "I don't know, Innocence. I will need to examine her and take some blood samples before I can tell you what is wrong with her. I think she was treated once at the hospital for tuberculosis."

Innocence wondered how the doctor could remember his mother's visit to the hospital. Then in a shaky voice he said, "Some others in our village had TB and died, but people said it was the other disease, AIDS, that really killed them. Could my mother have AIDS?"

The doctor looked at Innocence. "A person does not die from AIDS but dies because AIDS destroys the body's ability to fight other diseases. It is possible that that is what happened to the other people in your village, and it is possible that your mother may have AIDS. We can't know for sure until we test her blood."

The doctor saw the concerned look on the boy's face and added, "There is hope now for people with AIDS. We have a new program at the hospital that provides medicine for people with HIV infections. This new medicine allows people to live for a much longer time with the disease. If your mother is tested for HIV and is positive, she may qualify for this program."

As they drove into his village, Innocence felt a sense of relief for the first time in months. He was worried that his mother had AIDS, but, like so many Zambians, he did not mention his fears or talk about the awful disease. Until this moment, AIDS equaled death in Innocence's mind. Now, he had learned that there is hope for people with AIDS and maybe for his mother.

The doctor helped him open the Land Rover's door, and Innocence led the way to his mother's home.

24

Maji Ni Uhai

Maggie Montgomery

"Maju Ni Uhai" *is about Amani, a girl living in a rural village in Tanzania, and addresses the important role water plays in her life. In many African villages it takes time to collect water, especially during the dry season. Many villages do not have water pumps or wells, so they must collect water from nearby streams and rivers; the precious water that is collected can then turn out to be contaminated and cause diseases like typhoid and trachoma.*

Water is life. No one ever told Amani that water is life, or *maji ni uhai*, as is said in Swahili, the national language of Tanzania where Amani lives. Amani simply knows that her life (and possibly the future of her village) depends on water. Amani, the Swahili word for peace, lives in a colorful village near the shores of Lake Malawi in the far southwest corner of Tanzania, a nation in East Africa. The area where Amani lives is considered quite poor, even by Tanzanian standards. Tanzania is a poor country; many people survive on only one dollar each day. Amani's community does not have piped water, electricity, paved roads, or even a bridge to cross the mighty Ruhuhu River that separates Amani's village from the neighboring community and the health center.

On most mornings, the day begins with the intense sun rising over the quiet village. Amani usually watches the bright ball of fire creep above the horizon while she walks to the well early in the morning. By 7 AM sweat is pouring down Amani's face as she uses her small, strong arms to methodically pump, up and down, the water from the shallow well into the plastic yellow bucket she carries from home. "Amani, can't you pump any faster?" shout her friends waiting to collect water for their families. Amani responds with an African proverb her grandmother taught her. "*Pole, pole nydio mwendo,*" she says, meaning "slow, slow is the way to go." However, she does try to hurry and pump harder. School begins in just one hour, and she still has to walk over a mile home and then another two miles to school. It is the dry season; the water in the ground is no longer being replaced by rainwater seeping through the soil. Even pumping as hard as her arms will allow, only a small dribble comes out of the pump. Finally the bucket is full and just as she is about to heave the load onto her small head, she feels something smack her in the knee.

"Amani, you're it!" her friends yell as they throw the ball, which is actually a tightly bundled mass of plastic sacks tied together with string. Amani knows she does not have time for games, but she cannot resist. She picks up the ball, leaps along the smooth dirt that surrounds the well, and hurls it at her friend Rehima. She misses and instead hits Mama Queen's large behind. Mama yelps and frowns at Amani. Amani sheepishly apologizes and offers her the respectful greeting for elders: "*Shikamoo.*" Mama Queen silently accepts the apology but still frowns with annoyance. Amani bows her head and walks back to the yellow bucket of water.

Heaving the load onto her *kanga*, the carefully rolled cloth placed atop her head, Amani struggles not to spill any of the precious liquid. Rehima helps her position the bucket so it balances perfectly on her head, and then Amani begins the walk along the dirt trail that weaves past mango and coconut trees toward home. On reaching her family's mud hut, Amani slowly pours the water into a clay pot carefully designed to keep the water clean. She remembers learning from local health workers that clean water from a well can easily become contaminated with germs called pathogens before it is consumed. The contamination may be caused by many things, such as using unclean buckets, people putting their dirty hands and utensils into the water, or animals trying to drink from the bucket. Even the water taken from the well or the other places Amani goes to fetch water, such as Ruhuhu River, may be contaminated. Amani shudders as she remembers that whoever drinks water with pathogens in it is at risk of becoming sick and could even die. After pouring the water into the pot, her mother says, "Amani, make sure to put the lid on. We do not want the chickens and dogs helping themselves to our water."

Amani goes to change into her blue and white school uniform. She takes great care of her uniform; she is meticulous about not getting it dirty or ripping any holes in the sleeves. She knows it is the only uniform she will have for the entire year. After dressing, she walks over to the small cot, made of local reeds, to greet her sick sister, Upendo. She looks into her sister's eyes and squeezes her hand to let her know she is there. "Upendo," she whispers, "I love you and hope you will be healthy again soon."

Upendo, named after the word for love, is usually the most energetic and cheerful member of the family, but now her face is pale. Her eyes can barely stay open. She is suffering from typhoid. No one is exactly sure how Upendo became sick. She could have been exposed to the typhoid pathogen from drinking dirty water, not washing her hands before eating or after using the latrine, or even from flies that are known to spread diarrheal diseases. Luckily Amani's mother took Upendo to the local health clinic to obtain medication.

Even though Upendo is sick and other members of her family have suffered from diarrhea in the past, Amani's family does not always practice good hygiene. According to the village proverb, *Mungu atupeleka mgonjwa*, or God is the deliverer of illness. Even though her family knows that by washing their hands or boiling water they will prevent the harmful pathogens that cause disease from contaminating their water, it is difficult to always practice such behavior. Sometimes there is not enough firewood to boil water before drinking. At the latrine it is not customary to have a bucket of water nearby for washing.

After sitting for some time with her sister, Amani hears her mother shout, "You are going to be late. You need to get going, Amani!" Amani bolts out the door and dashes toward school. She runs the entire way, because she knows how upset her teacher gets when she is late. Once she arrives, she is nearly an hour late and exhausted. Before heading into the classroom, she takes a minute to wash her face. Standing beneath the large gourd filled with water, she lets the cool water spills over her eyes and face. Last year the school instituted a face washing program to help prevent trachoma, a potentially blinding disease linked to poor hygiene and lack of sanitation. Now every day, before and after school, the children, including Amani, wash their faces.

Amani wipes the water from her face and walks into the classroom, crossing her fingers for luck. Her teacher, Bibi Elimu, can be frightfully strict. Luckily today Bibi is in a good mood. "Amani, as I have told you, lateness is not acceptable. If you want to learn and escape the confines of poverty, you need an education. I will not punish you this time, but this is your last warning."

Amani breathes a sigh of relief for only receiving a verbal reminder that lateness is frowned on. She sits down on the dirt floor, squeezing between a few of her friends in the crowded classroom. The school cannot afford desks or basic supplies such as workbooks. Amani tries to listen attentively as the teacher explains the importance of practicing good health, but it is easy to become distracted with so many kids sitting so close together. Just as Amani begins to daydream, Bibi calls on her, "Amani can you give us an example of good hygiene?"

Amani thinks for a moment and replies, "After using the latrine you should wash your hands and before eating a meal as well. It is also important to use soap to kill germs." Amani knows that many traditional customs can easily spread pathogens and increase risks for disease. For instance, in Tanzania people commonly eat with their fingers and share food from one large plate in the center of the table. This practice has existed for centuries, long before individuals could afford to purchase silverware. Even now Amani's family and community continues to eat from one plate, sharing in the bounty of the earth and making sure no one goes unfed. With so many hands on one plate it is especially easy to spread germs.

Bibi Elimu goes on to explain the need to kill pathogens and improve water quality before drinking it. "We can make our water safer to drink through many methods," she states. "Some of these include boiling water over a fire, putting water in plastic bottles and leaving them in the sun for a day, adding chemicals such as chlorine, or even pouring the water through clay filters to remove and absorb some of the harmful pathogens." Amani listens carefully to what Bibi Elimu says and is perplexed by what the village elders say about God bringing illnesses and what she hears now. Amani wonders which belief is true, whether it is God or dirty water that brings illnesses or if both could be correct. Her thoughts are interrupted by Bibi Elimu announcing that the next lesson, history, is about to begin.

"Today we are going to discuss the Maji Maji Rebellion," Bibi Elimu exclaims, raising her voice so all the children can hear. "Can anyone tell me about the rebellion?" The children squirm and, hoping to avoid being called on, try not to make eye contact with their teacher. After an uncomfortable silence, Bibi Elimu goes on to explain that, "The Maji Maji Rebellion was an uprising that took place over one hundred years ago in an area just north of here. At the time the Germans ruled Tanzania. A famous African chief began a rebellion to force the colonialists to leave so Tanzanians could have freedom. He recruited villagers to fight by telling them if they used a special potion he had created, the German bullets would turn into *maji*, or water. With this story about the potion he was able to get thousands of villagers who did not have modern weapons to fight against the Germans. When the battle took place, the Germans fired with their guns and thousands of Tanzanians were killed." Amani suddenly raises her hand and asks, "If water is life, why did the potion not turn the bullets to water?" Bibi Elimu responds, "That is a good question, Amani. Sometimes our traditions are not enough to overcome the scientific laws of nature."

The school day is now over. Amani, along with a swarm of her friends, rushes outside into the bright, radiant sun. She walks along the dirt path toward home, skipping and singing. It takes over an hour to reach home, but she does not mind. The time allows her to play and enjoy the end of the day.

As Amani reaches her family's hut, she rushes inside to see if her sister's health has improved. Unfortunately her condition has worsened throughout the day. Upendo's forehead is even warmer now than it was in the morning. Her fever and the infection are getting worse. Amani hugs Upendo's weak body. "Mama, have you given Upendo the medicine the doctor prescribed?"

"Yes, Amani, but sometimes even medicine cannot provide a cure," her mother replies.

Amani nods her head in agreement. She knows that water is life, *maji ni uhai*, and hopes that her sister will one day soon be at the well with her pumping water, playing games, and continuing to live life as best one can in her Tanzanian village.

25

The Open Door

Nicole Warren

"The Open Door" describes Sali's role as a midwife in rural Burkina Faso. In many countries, there are few health professionals available, especially ones who can provide care during childbirth. Sali—the only midwife in her village—gives essential care to the women in her community and is able to identify births that are in trouble and need medical attention. In this story, Sali delivers her close friend Fatime's baby; the birth is a dangerous one, requiring Sali to seek medical assistance in the nearby city.

Sali felt Issa squirming on her back, impatiently signaling to be taken off to relieve himself. *He will have to wait a few moments*, she thought. Sali would have to fill the last buckets with water before she had enough to last the rest of the evening. If she postponed retrieving the water, then there might not be time later. She squinted through the falling sun's rays and saw her sister, sister-in-law, and best friend walk by her compound's entrance.

"You and the afternoon," they called in unison.

"You and the afternoon," she replied with a soft smile.

"The door is open," her sister called happily. Sali looked up at her sister with an anxious expression. Her sister was referring to the huge metal door of the village maternity. An open door meant that someone was having a baby.

"I know, I know," Sali responded hurriedly, dropping the black plastic satchel deep into the well for the last time. Sali picked up the last two buckets of water with her baby Issa on her back, knowing that she had a long evening ahead.

Fatime felt the pains again and again, gripping her belly and hips like a vice. She tried not to think about what old women said about a woman in labor. That she would have one foot on earth, the other in the grave. Instead, she focused on her mother's hushed words of advice. It had been three days since the first twinges of pain. The pain was searing now, demanding her full attention. It was Fatime's first pregnancy, and she feared the pressure inside her hips would never end.

In preparation of her visit to the maternity, Sali gathered her things in the dwindling light, stepping over empty syringes and glass ampoules from the floor of her hut. It had become almost impossible to keep the syringes' bright yellow plastic wrappers separate from her calabashes of flour and grain. As Sali reached for her prepared bag, Issa kicked his foot in the air—barely missing her forehead—and giggled. She looked up and smiled.

In the few short months since she had become the village midwife, Sali's life had changed significantly. The same week Sali received her midwifery certificate from the health center, she became a mother. Thankfully, the old village midwife, who had learned midwifery from the midwife before her, agreed to help her. Today, she thought of the old midwife's practices and the ways midwifery had changed since her mother gave birth. The old village midwife had successfully delivered many babies, but Sali knew that the skills she'd acquired in her training would improve the health of the women in her village. Each year, too many women died in childbirth from preventable causes.

Lost in thought, Sali reached to pick up Issa as he extended his legs, howling in protest and trying to writhe away from the warm stool. "Eh Allah!" she cried as she untangled the soiled cloth from Issa's chubby legs. Now they would both need a bath before she could leave. It was too much sometimes, being new at so many things.

On the second day, the cramps that crossed Fatime's belly moved to the inside of her small hips. When the pressure started to feel uncomfortable, her mother-in-law smirked and said with confidence, "You will soon bring my first grandchild into the world."

Yet, hours later there was still no baby. Fatime looked up at her mother-in-law who fanned herself impatiently; the heat was becoming unbearable. The old woman disappeared and Fatime was left alone with the heat. Her mother-in-law returned with herbs and made a tea for Fatime, assuring her that it would cool her fever. However, the tea did not break her fever and the fluid leaking from her body grew foul—so foul that her mother-in-law finally gave in and agreed to bring her to labor at the maternity. Fatime knew that her husband had had a successful cotton crop this year because he had bought a new bike; she knew they could afford a trip to the maternity.

Sali was relieved when Issa's head fell against her back in exhaustion. She carefully slipped him off her back and onto a bamboo mat outside her hut. It was still warm enough to sleep outside, so she laid a towel over his head to keep the mosquitoes at bay. Sali dutifully put her lab coat on over her clean skirt and blouse and worked to ignore her husband's stare. He was unhappy with the hours she worked: this was the third night in a row she had neglected to warm his water for bathing and prepare his dinner. When she was first chosen to train as the village midwife, he was proud. She was the only young woman in their village who had completed six years of formal education and could read and write; the promise of a prestigious job and a regular salary had excited him. Yet, he underestimated the amount of time this job would require and began to resent her. However, Sali was proud of her education and midwifery skills. And she knew that the community really needed her.

Sali said good-bye to her husband and quickly crossed the well-worn path to the maternity building. Even in the dim moonlight, she walked confidently, occasionally dodging the muddy puddles left from last week's heavy rains. She held on to her new delivery kit tightly with her right hand. Her new delivery kit was filled with the medicines and medical equipment she would need for the birth; she received the delivery kit from a nonprofit organization that had provided training in the city—but she was unsure how she would replace the items once she'd used them. Sali had asked the organization to come to her village to train other women home-based lifesaving skills, but their limited time prevented them from visiting. She had heard of some programs providing maternal health training, but she had never heard of one in her area. Midwives in the rural areas of Burkino Faso often received less attention than midwives in urban areas.

Regardless, Sali had enough supplies to cover this birth and knew she couldn't panic until her supplies ran out. Sali knew the women in her village couldn't pay for medical supplies—it was difficult enough to get them to come to the maternity to deliver their babies. Left to their own devices, they would deliver at home. She sighed heavily and picked up her feet to a brisk walk. She hoped to increase the number of women who delivered under her care, but this would be hard to do without education, and finding time to hold education sessions with the women of her village would be difficult. The women were busy. *She* was busy. For now, it was all she could do to keep up with her own household and tend to the labors she could.

As Sali entered the maternity courtyard, she saw an old woman drawing water from the well. Every expecting mother brought an elder woman—usually her mother-in-law—with her to help her through the labor. Sali still felt uncomfortable telling the elders what to do—the older women of the village had attended many more births than she had.

"You and the night, Sali!" the old woman greeted her joyfully.

"You and the night, wise woman," Sali responded. "She's OK?" Sali couldn't resist asking.

"It's coming too slow, Sali." She paused and smiled. "But I'm sure a little girl like you can handle it." The old woman had known Sali since she was a baby. Sali and Fatime had grown up together. Sali glanced back at the old woman who now stoked the fire. Her muscles were clear under her wrinkled, sagging skin. It was true, she had seen much more of life than Sali.

Sali approached the open maternity door. Dim lantern lights shone through the windows and cast shadows across the courtyard. The old village midwife had never complained about the light, as she was accustomed to working in near darkness. But when Sali became the midwife, she had asked the village council for better lights, like the ones she had used during her training. Fortunately, a foreign volunteer agency had installed a solar panel, which provided a large fluorescent light to ease her work at night. But the panel is broken at the moment, so she will have to rely on the lanterns tonight.

Sali slid her flip-flops off at the doorway and walked toward the delivery room. The room was simple but clean. Sali was proud of her two twin bed frames, delivery table, and wood desk. Not every midwife had so much furniture. She hoped the village council would be able to buy mattresses soon.

Fatime was on her knees, swaying her hips side to side. Sali could tell the contraction was ending because Fatime's eyelids relaxed, and her clenched jaw dropped in relief. Sali settled her things on the desk and watched Fatime rest her head on her forearm and settle her hips over her ankles.

"You and the night," Sali greeted her, when Fatime had a moment of rest.

"You and the night," Fatime responded. The greeting was standard but the gasp that followed it was revealing. As the next pain came, Fatime bolted up on her knees and sucked air in through her clenched teeth. Her voice became low as the pain peaked, and Sali knew Fatime was pushing. This was a good sign.

When the contraction ended, Sali had Fatime climb onto the table. The old metal delivery table was salvaged from a clinic in the city. To Sali, the table was an awkward place to examine women, but she used it anyway. The village women expected her to use the delivery table, just like they expected her to administer an IV and medicines to make labor go faster. Sali knew that the medicines lured women to her clinic. If Sali didn't use her resources, she might be accused of not doing her job.

Sali took a dry exam glove from the clothes line that ran across the delivery room. She had learned about HIV and AIDS during her midwifery training, and so she always wore gloves. She cleaned them after each use and hung them to dry—she had to treat them with care because she only had ten of them. She slipped on a glove and examined Fatime, who was now dilated nine centimeters. She needed to dilate ten centimeters to deliver. Because of the long labor, Sali worried that Fatime's womb could have become infected. She quickly reached for her wooden fetoscope, the handmade instrument that allowed her to listen to the baby's heart beat. She was relieved to hear it was strong.

"How long have you been having pains?" Sali asked as she helped Fatime off the table.

"Three days," Fatime responded breathlessly.

"Two!" Fatime's mother-in-law interjected her own assessment. "It wasn't bad the first day, so that doesn't count!" Her voice having been heard, the old lady plopped down on the bare springs of one of the old bed frames and crossed her arms.

Given how long Fatime had been in labor, Sali was relieved that she was nine centimeters dilated. Sali quickly spread out the worn black plastic tarp used for deliveries. As directed, Fatime pushed with the next few contractions, crawling or lying down on the tarp between pains.

An hour later, Fatime was completely dilated, and Sali instructed Fatime to push harder with every pain. Fatime, desperate by this point, said she could not go on. Sali looked at her friend and said, "Now you must push!" The assertive direction sounded odd coming from the young midwife, as though she herself was not convinced of the advice.

After another hour or so, Sali saw the baby's head, but she knew it was taking too long. She listened for the baby's heart rate and noticed that it slowed down after each contraction, a sign that it was stressed by all the effort. For the next few contractions, Sali knelt above Fatime's head and used the palms of her hands to push the top of Fatime's belly as hard as she could in the direction of her feet. She had seen the old village midwife do this to help force the baby out. She could think of no other solution.

Fatime screamed in protest but was overwhelmed by the stretching and burning below. Sali caught the baby as its head and then body emerged. Fatime collapsed against her mother-in-law and closed her eyes, relieved. Sali carefully tied and cut the umbilical cord with her last clean razor blade. As Fatime caught her breath, she self-consciously closed her knees.

"It's a girl. No wonder she gave you so much trouble!" Sali said to Fatime. The two childhood friends shared a quick laugh.

Fatime raised her head to take a first peek at her child. She looked concerned by the baby's wailing, but Sali knew that this was a good thing. The baby's crying turned her skin pink, and Sali relaxed for a moment. Sali cleaned and wrapped the baby, handing her to her grandmother for a more complete assessment. Sali's own niece appeared in the doorway.

"He's hungry," she said, patting Issa's squirming bottom through the cloth that held him on her back. She had brought Issa to Sali so she could breastfeed her son.

"Give him to me," Sali said. She had a few minutes before Fatime's placenta, the afterbirth, would come out. She removed her gloves and washed her hands quickly in the water she had collected. In a few fluid movements she raised her blouse and started feeding Issa. She felt her shoulders relax as Issa began to nurse. She was exhausted.

A few minutes later, Issa was contently asleep at her breast. Sali was anxious to finish now—the placenta had not come out on its own. She handed Issa back to her niece. "Take him home," she directed. "I'll be there soon." The young girl swaddled Issa on her back and disappeared into the dark courtyard.

Sali saw that Fatime looked pale and was surrounded by dark, fresh blood. Sali called the old woman to bring the lantern closer. Kneeling near Fatime, Sali tugged on the cord gently and massaged Fatime's belly. The placenta still did not come. Fatime did not stop bleeding. Fatime was drowsy and closed her eyes—Sali noticed that the puddle was extending to the edges of her black plastic tarp.

"We need oxytocin," Sali said out loud, knowing that the drug could speed labor up but it could also stop bleeding afterward. Suddenly, she remembered the pharmacy was out of oxytocin. She knew that the only other solution was to get Fatime to the city. It would take twenty minutes on a fast moped.

"Get her husband. Now!" Sali barked at the old woman.

"Why? She's just tired," the old woman said offhandedly. She didn't take Fatime seriously.

"No, it's too much, she shouldn't be so quiet. Get him now!" The old woman looked startled by the authority in Sali's voice. The old woman got up and shuffled off into the dark. Sali sat with Fatime and tried to extract the placenta a couple more times without success. Fatime's breath was fast and shallow, but Sali could feel her own heart racing.

"Fatime! Fatime!" She seemed to be fighting sleep now, rolling her head from side to side. Sali impatiently mopped up the floor until she heard a young man's voice call from the doorway.

"You and the night. You called me?" he said hesitantly.

Sali cried out impatiently, "Yes, yes. Do you have a moped? Your wife needs to go to the city for medicine. She's bleeding too much."

There was a long pause and Sali looked up at the tin roof for what seemed like an eternity.

"No, but my father does. I'll have to ask him." Fatime's husband disappeared into the night, and Sali heard his footsteps across the muddy courtyard. She returned to Fatime, turning her onto her side, which is the best position for a woman who bleeds too much. Fatime looked peaceful now and the baby slept on the bed frame a few feet away. Sali checked the placenta again. No luck. Only this time, the bleeding was worse when she massaged Fatime's belly. Sali knew that this was a hemorrhage: just what she feared. "Please, please," Sali found herself praying, "make it stop, make it stop!"

"Fatime, Fatime!" Sali called. Fatime didn't respond. She held her face in her hand and moved it back and forth. Nothing except fast, shallow breaths. The old woman came back inside, and Sali instructed her to take care of the baby, because she was taking Fatime to the city for medicine to stop the bleeding. The old woman huffed, "Oh, Sali, you know what they do to women there. They'll try to cut her open! Leave her be." Sali was speechless. *Couldn't she see what needed to be done?*

The moped puttered into the courtyard and broke the silence. The engine cut out and the man's voice was at the door again, more urgent now. "My father says we can use it, but there isn't much gas." Sali could tell from his voice that he was scared. Sali rolled Fatime off the tarp and tried to wrap her in the last of the dry clothes. She called Fatime's husband in to help her, but he entered hesitantly. The maternity was not a man's place.

"Help me, I can't move her by myself!" Sali tried to keep her panic out of her voice. The two struggled awkwardly with Fatime; her body was heavy and quiet now. They carried her toward the doorway to the moped. They struggled to arrange both Sali and Fatime on the narrow rack behind the driver's seat. Fatime's body was listless and Sali fought to keep her upright. The old woman spoke up from the doorway.

"It's too late, Sali. It's the truth. Just clean her now so her body can rest." Sali responded, "There is medicine for this—we have to try to save her." She signaled to Fatime's husband, and the three of them disappeared into the night.

The threesome made it to the city's health center while it was still dark. The midwives at the big maternity eyed them suspiciously from the entrance. They didn't like villagers arriving in such disarray. Village midwives were known for coming too late or not at all.

"It was her first baby. The placenta never came out. She's lost a lot of blood and she's not responding anymore." The story rushed out of Sali's mouth with a confidence she barely recognized. She had always felt intimidated by the big maternity. She knew they didn't trust village midwives. The staff just watched Sali and Fatime's husband struggle to get Fatime inside to a bed.

"Why didn't you bring her earlier?" the head midwife barked as she moved next to Fatime and took her blood pressure and pulse. Sali braced herself. "I brought her as soon as I could. We didn't have any oxytocin in the village."

"Well, if you're lucky, we'll be able to start a blood transfusion before she dies." The head midwife directed her attention to another midwife. "Go wake up Dr. Ouedraogo. He needs to see this one. She's had a terrible hemorrhage."

A few minutes later, the doctor arrived and approved the blood transfusion and they also started an IV line with extra fluids. Sali saw that the vital signs were improving, and she began to feel better. The head midwife took Sali aside. "You know, she was almost dead when you brought her here." She put her arm on Sali's shoulders. "She would have never made it if you hadn't come." With that, she returned to tend to Fatime.

Sali insisted Fatime's husband drive her home. She knew she had to return before morning to tend to Issa and her husband. They arrived at the entrance to her family's compound just before dawn. Before going back to the city to tend to his wife, Fatime's husband said, "May God give you great gifts."

Sali smiled tiredly and turned into the entrance of her home. Inside, Sali found Issa beside her niece, still sleeping on the bamboo mat. Sali laid down next to him and closed her eyes, savoring the few precious moments of sleep before she would need to start her chores.

26

The Accident

Kenneth Maes and Gabriel Okpattah

"The Accident" tells the story of Jacob, a Ghanaian boy committed to overcoming the obstacles life presents him, including the consequences of a terrible traffic accident. Traffic accidents are one of the biggest killers worldwide. Countries like Ghana that have poor infrastructure and underfunded hospitals have fewer resources to treat injuries from traffic accidents. Jacob realizes that traffic accidents and illnesses like AIDS have something in common—neither are really "accidents." Because most Ghanaians are poor, they are at greater risk for many things that could put them in the hospital, from serious injuries to serious infections. And once there, they can't always expect good treatment. Jacob's hospital stay took all the money he had saved, and he still didn't get the necessary operation to fix his leg.

"Jacob, I'm home! Guess what? I got the job! Your own brother is now the assistant stockboy at the new alcohol distillery down the road!"

"Joseph, are you serious?! Now we can pay the house rent! Hey, why don't we celebrate? Too bad you didn't bring home a bottle of your company's product."

Joseph knew Jacob was kidding about the alcohol, but he raised his eyebrows and said, "Jake, just because I'm working at the alcohol distillery doesn't mean we are going to start drinking that stuff."

"Hmm. Well, I guess I just wish you were going to work for the water distillery—it's hard enough for us to get good water to drink," Jacob said as he realized he hadn't had any water all day. The sun, which seems a bit bigger on the equator, was just dipping below the rooftops in the brothers' neighborhood, finally giving some relief from the heat.

"Well, at least I'll bring home some money at the end of the month. We can use it to get water and food," Joseph said with hunger and thirst in his eyes. "Maybe even buy bus tickets to visit grandfather after the rainy season." Joseph was thinking back to the days when he and Jacob lived with their grandfather and aunts. Their grandfather once told them that back in his early days, nobody used money. People traded the different foods they produced, and nobody went hungry.

"I promise that the alcohol won't come home with me. If it wasn't for alcohol, mom and dad might still be around, and your leg wouldn't be broken . . ."

"Ah, forget about my leg," Jacob said, as he patted his brother on the back. "Let's be thankful we are both alive. I'm going to get some egg sandwiches for dinner. Want to come?"

As the two brothers walked down the dirt road to the corner where the women sell sandwiches each night, Jacob became lost in his thoughts. When he and Joseph were in fifth grade, their father lost his job with the Volta River Authority, where he worked constructing Ghana's first hydroelectric dam. That was when their father started drinking. When money became scarce, their mother began selling corn dough and cassava balls in the market and on the street. At the end of the school day, Jacob and Joseph often went to the market to sell with her. Jacob remembers how their mother showed them how to carry the baskets of corn dough on their heads as they sold the cassava balls.

This didn't support Jacob's family for long. The brothers were forced to move to Keta, a small coastal town on the Gulf of Guinea, to live with their grandfather. After enrolling Jacob and Joseph in the local school, their parents returned to Accra to find work. Every afternoon after school in Keta, Jacob and Joseph helped the fishermen drag their nets in from the sea. Pulling in one net could take two hours in the hot sun, even with twenty people helping. They often brought home fish at the end of the day, and their aunts would cook up some spicy stew for dinner.

When they completed junior high school, the twins left their grandfather in Keta and moved back to Accra to find their parents. But they didn't like what they found in Accra. Their parents had divorced and their father had begun drinking heavily. He was not the man they once looked up to.

All of a sudden Jacob came out of his thoughts. He and Joseph were by this time eating their egg sandwiches, staring quietly at the setting sun. "Joseph, promise me you won't bring alcohol home. Leave it at work."

Joseph knew Jacob was thinking about their father. "I promise, Jake," he replied.

Joseph often reminds Jacob of his broken leg, as if it were a symbol of their struggle to survive. Jacob tries not to think about it too much. It was just last year, about this time, that he had the accident.

One morning, Jacob was traveling toward downtown Accra in a minibus taxi to buy some music at the wholesale market. Jacob had a little money to spend that he had earned from the extra shifts he was working to save up for school fees at the University of Ghana. He had recently graduated from St. Peter's Preparatory. He had attended the school on a scholarship and graduated from it with honors. At St. Peter's, his classmates called him "Justice Boy" because he was so often reading about Dr. Martin Luther King Jr. and Nelson Mandela, and he didn't allow anyone to step on someone else's rights.

Jacob was riding downtown in one of the local minibuses that take passengers from junction to junction. The vast majority of people in Accra take crowded minibuses around town, while wealthier people have their own cars or take private taxis. Minibuses sometimes had sixteen people inside, and a passenger might share her space with bags of rice, yams, or even chickens. Even though he was small, Jacob's knees still jammed up against the seats in front of him. There are no seatbelts, and the seats are barely even bolted down. Sometimes Jacob can see the pavement rushing by through holes in the floor. And of course, the drivers are always in a hurry, cutting every corner so close that one wonders why accidents don't happen more often.

When Jacob got into the minibus that morning, he thought the driver smelled a bit like alcohol. He looked down at the driver's feet and saw an empty bottle rolling around. On the way to town, the driver swerved and the minibus suddenly tilted on two wheels. Jacob remembers the noise of screeching tires as the bus began to roll over. Jacob also heard the sounds of people screaming in horror and pain. But at that point, Jacob blacked out.

The people who rushed to the accident didn't know if Jacob was alive. After the accident, Jacob was taken to the hospital. He wasn't even breathing. A witness who knew him went and called his brother and told him, "I think Jacob is dead." Joseph rushed to the hospital and checked the "dead list," but his name was not there. He couldn't find Jacob at the morgue, either.

After some hours, Jacob woke up from his coma. His heart began to race, and all he could think was, *Where am I?* The nurse told him to calm down. "You are lucky to be alive," she said. She told him that he'd been in an accident, and all of a sudden he started to remember taking the minibus. He checked his pockets and discovered that his money was missing. The nurse told him again to relax. She gave him a couple of injections and left the room.

Jacob was so afraid. He tried to stand up. He had broken his leg, so he was holding it up. He fell back into bed, and now his mind began to race. He thought about his parents and his brother Joseph, and he wondered if his leg was going to be OK. His leg looked like it was dead.

He wasn't going to stay in that bed. He managed to escape the hospital room by holding the walls.

Jacob expected hospitals to be white, bright, and clean. But this place was not like that at all, even though it was one of the biggest public hospitals in Accra. He couldn't tell which way led out of the building. He ended up going through a pair of doors without any sign. He soon realized that he had entered the ward that cares for patients living with AIDS. Many of Jacob's neighbors are poor, and he had seen plenty of thin and sick-looking people on the street—people living with polio, HIV, and many other illnesses. Jacob knew about AIDS. He knew the facts about who is at risk and knew that people living with this disease need care. But he was overwhelmed by the bedridden people he saw in this room. There were fathers, mothers, and children looking so thin. Those who were not asleep looked scared, more scared than he felt.

Jacob woke up one of the men and asked him if there were any nurses around.

"I haven't seen any. But if you find one, please let her know that Maggie here has a very high fever. And tell her I want to telephone my son." As Jacob looked at Maggie, intending to introduce himself, she turned away, hiding her face and her sad, feverish eyes. Jacob told the man he would notify a nurse if he found one and turned around to leave. The man stopped him, "What is your name? You broke your leg?"

"My name is Jacob Gavua. And yes, I think it is broken."

"Your name is familiar. Did your dad work with the Volta River Authority?"

"Yes, that was my father," Jacob answered excitedly. "He helped to construct the dam."

"I used to work with him. My name is Mr. Prempeh. Your father was a hard worker. We both were," the man said as his eyes drifted back toward sleep. "You take care of your leg. You'll have to work harder to survive now, but don't let it keep you down."

"I will try. And I hope you get better, too." But Mr. Prempeh was already asleep.

Jacob made it out of the hospital, still without any doctor or nurse stopping him. There was a telecom center within the hospital compound. A man took his number and got Joseph on the line. Joseph asked him if a miracle had happened. Once Jacob got his brother to calm down, he told him, "Listen, I can't be here in the hospital. I'm scared for my life."

So Joseph came to the hospital and paid for the call. Without telling anyone, they left for home. Joseph helped Jacob get into his bunk bed, and they fell asleep. At dawn, Jacob awoke with intense pain in his leg. It was unbearable, and he started to regret leaving the hospital. They rushed back to the hospital on another minibus taxi. The nurses complained—"Where did you go? We were looking for you!" They were angry. They said, "You could be dead! You see how much pain you have?"

Jacob stayed in the hospital for two weeks, but his leg has never stopped hurting. He hasn't been able to work since the accident, and it took several months of searching for his brother Joseph to finally find a better job.

After the twins finished eating their egg sandwiches and had gotten back home, they climbed into their bunk beds. Jacob opened the book he was reading. Joseph put his headphones over his ears and started listening to one of his favorite local bands. Within about ten minutes, both had drifted to sleep.

Jacob would tell you that the minibus accident changed his life. He often thinks about how he could have been hospitalized for a different reason. He could be one of the people he saw dying in that hospital ward. He thinks about Mr. Prempeh, who wanted to telephone his son. Jacob could tell that Mr. Prempeh just wanted to talk to somebody. He also thinks about Maggie, who never said a word and hid her face. Jacob wishes he could have told her not to feel ashamed.

Jacob has not let his broken leg defeat him. He took Mr. Prempeh's advice and applied to become a university student. When Jacob begins his studies at the University of Ghana, he will still take a minibus back and forth between his home in the slums and the university campus. Living in these poor conditions means a bad decision or a little stroke of bad luck could put himself, his brother, or his friends in the hospital, or worse. But with some hard work, good luck, and hope, he knows he can stay healthy and complete his studies.

27

Mr. Coulibaly's Advice

Amy Patterson

"Mr. Coulibaly's Advice" is about Adama, a young boy living in a village in Mali, and the importance of being educated about malaria to fight it. Malaria is a disease transmitted to human beings by mosquitoes. It is uncommon in the United States but is one of the most dangerous diseases worldwide. It is one of the major killers of children. This narrative introduces different types of approaches to healing. In some cases, traditional remedies may be successful, but in other cases, pharmaceutical medicines are essential.

"I bet you can't hit that bird with your slingshot," Seydou taunted, pointing to a small bird with long iridescent blue feathers.

Seydou and Adama were supposed to be on their way to school, but they had decided to take a detour through the mango grove to collect some of the large green fruits tinted with red and yellow that dangled from long stems, just out of reach of their outstretched hands. Seydou had tied his knife to a long wooden pole and was attempting to cut the stem of a ripe and juicy mango when he saw the bird resting in a nearby tree.

Unable to resist the challenge, Adama picked up his slingshot and a small stone. He fit the stone to the slingshot, stretched the black rubber band until it was tight, gauged the position of the bird—and finally released the stone. Without a sound, the bird fell from its branch on the tree. Seydou abandoned his quest for the perfectly ripe mango and ran to look at the fallen bird. Adama, however, stood still, the slingshot forgotten in his hand. As soon as the stone left his slingshot, he had begun to regret his action. Feeling very guilty, he turned and started walking toward the school, leaving his friend standing over the unlucky prey. He no longer had any desire to pick mangoes, no matter how sweet and ripe they were.

Adama was already late for class when he arrived at the small school in Tonfa, a small village in the southern region of the West African country of Mali. The school was a one-room building made of earthen bricks with a straw roof. He walked in and took his seat on one of the long wooden benches on the boys' side of the classroom. Seydou arrived a few seconds later, out of breath from running. The teacher was already standing at the blackboard, and he directed a disapproving look in the boys' direction, a warning of the punishment to come if they were late again.

The teacher, Mr. Coulibaly, turned back to the lesson: health. On the board Mr. Coulibaly had written "sumaya," which is the Bambara word for malaria. Next to that, he had written "le paludisme," which is the French word for malaria. The teacher explained that *sumaya* is a sickness that is caused by a small creature that lives in the blood. When a mosquito bites a person who is infected with *sumaya* and then bites another person, it can give *sumaya* to the second person. He told the students that the symptoms of *sumaya* include *farikalaya* (a hot body or fever), *kungolodimi* (headache), and a lack of appetite. If it is a very serious case, then the symptoms can also include *kônô* (convulsions) and *jè* (pale skin). The teacher then told the students that people who are sick with *sumaya* should go to the community health center immediately to get treatment. If not treated, people can die from malaria. He also said that people can protect themselves from *sumaya* by sleeping under mosquito nets that have been treated with insecticide.

After the health lesson, it was time for the morning math lesson. This was Adama's favorite class, and by the time he had solved a particularly hard problem that the teacher had written on the board, he had forgotten all about the bird that was lying on the ground in the mango grove, its shiny blue feathers now covered with flies.

Several days later, when Adama returned home for lunch, he learned that his youngest sister, Fatoumata, was sick. Adama washed his hands, pouring water from the purple and yellow plastic teapot that the family used for that purpose since they didn't have running water. He sat down to eat, reaching his right hand into a large bowl of rice with peanut sauce. He looked longingly at the pieces of meat in the bowl of rice, but he knew that the meat was always saved for the men in his family who had been working in the fields all day. He returned his glance to the bowl of rice he was sharing with four of his brothers and sisters. He was initially glad that Fatoumata wasn't there, since that meant more food for him. However, as he listened to his mother and grandmother talk about his sister's illness, he began to worry.

His mother told his grandmother that Fatoumata had had *farikalaya* on and off for the past few days. Today, however, the illness had gotten worse. She had been crying all morning, she had refused to eat anything, and she had no interest in playing with her siblings. Adama's grandmother listened quietly and then said that she had seen this illness before. She advised Adama's mother to look for a certain plant in the forest, to boil it in water, and then to give some to Fatoumata to drink and use the rest to bathe her. If the illness is caused by something like dirty water or by eating too many mangoes, this treatment should cure it. However, Grandmother said with premonition, if Fatoumata starts to have *kônô*, we will know that the illness was not caused by natural causes and was instead caused by an evil spirit in the form of a bird. If that is the case, she explained, we need to go to a traditional healer so that he can treat the illness using spells that only he knows.

Adama listened carefully to his grandmother. She was the wisest person that he knew. She always offered him rational advice whenever he had a problem. His father talked to her whenever he had a fight with one of his three wives. His mother talked to her to learn how to prepare his father's favorite sauces. Everyone in the family went to his grandmother to learn which plants to use to treat their illnesses when they were sick. Adama remembered the bird in the mango grove and he began to wonder if he had angered the evil bird spirit that causes *kônô*. He worried that his little sister would suffer from his actions.

After washing his hands again, Adama went over to his sister who was lying on a brightly colored piece of fabric in the shade of a tree. He touched her arm and found that her skin was very hot. He tickled her gently. Usually she laughed when he did this, but today she didn't respond at all. As he stood by his sister, he remembered his teacher's lesson from a few days ago. His sister might have malaria, and if so, she would need to go to the health center for treatment—but his grand-mother had listed water, mangoes, and an evil spirit as causes of the illness. She hadn't mentioned anything about mosquitoes.

Adama decided to go and talk to his teacher. He found Mr. Coulibaly sitting in front of his house with several friends, watching a soccer match on TV. They had brought the television outside and had hooked it up to a car battery for power. The men were in the process of making the sweet green tea mixed with mint and sugar that is popular among Malian men. Mr. Coulibaly looked up from his tea making and saw Adama standing at the entrance to the yard. He gestured for Adama to come in.

Adama pulled up a small wooden stool and sat down next to Mr. Coulibaly. He explained that his little sister was sick and that he was confused because his grandmother's advice concerning the illness seemed to conflict with what Mr. Coulibaly had taught them in class. Mr. Coulibaly listened carefully. When he responded, the teacher told Adama that his grandmother was very wise and that the traditional medicines she recommended can be very effective for some illnesses. In fact, he told Adama, the medicines that the health center uses to treat malaria are made from plants traditionally used by wise elders like his grandmother. These plants, however, were not found in Mali, and thus it was necessary to go to the health center to get medicine to treat malaria. Mr. Coulibaly also explained that it was safer to use medicines from the health center because the necessary dosage could be measured exactly and because it eliminated the risk of mistaking a helpful plant for a harmful one.

Adama nodded but then told his teacher what was really troubling him. He confessed to killing the bird in the mango grove and asked his teacher if he could have caused his sister's illness. Mr. Coulibaly smiled.

"There are a lot of mysterious things that happen that no one can explain," he said. "I myself have heard of a man whose skin could not be cut, even with a very sharp knife. And I know a woman who paid a magician for a spell to prevent her husband from marrying a second wife. On the day of the wedding, the husband mysteriously left town without telling anyone. He came back a week after the wedding date, but by that time the other woman refused to marry him. However, when it comes to malaria, we do now know how to explain it. Scientists have been able to show that you get malaria when you are bitten by a mosquito that is infected with the illness."

The expression of relief on Adama's face was very clear.

"However," the teacher continued, "you shouldn't be killing birds just for pleasure. If you are going to eat them, that is one thing. But wasting a life is a terrible thing to do." Adama nodded and promised that he wouldn't do it again.

"Now," said Mr. Coulibaly, "go home and tell your father that I said that he should bring Fatoumata to the health center for medicine." "And," he called after the boy who was already on his way out the gate, "don't be late for school tomorrow!"

28

Amina Ndiaye

Charlotte Kvasnovsky

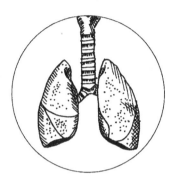

"Amina Ndiaye" tells the story of Amina, a girl living in Senegal, who is suffering from a tuberculosis infection. Amina's story is a happy one: not only is her tuberculosis caught early, but her family also happens to live near a medical clinic. She is treated quickly and completes the suggested course, which improves her health and clears her tuberculosis. This narrative highlights the importance of knowing what the symptoms of tuberculosis are and illustrates techniques for preventing it.

Amina Ndiaye is fifteen years old and lives with her mother and her two sisters in St. Louis, a city in the north of Senegal. They share a house with her mother's sister and her daughters. Both her father and her uncle spend most of the year in Kaolack working on peanut farms, which is located in the Peanut Basin, the low-laying area between the Ferlo and Gambia rivers.

Two streets away from Amina's house is the hospital. Amina's mom and her aunt cook at the hospital, preparing meals for the doctors and nurses. Each day they cook the traditional meal of fried rice with *thiebu dien*, a tasty recipe combining fish, onions, cassava, cabbage, eggplant, carrots, and a habanero pepper. Often, when people in Senegal get sick, family members accompany them to the hospital, and those family members make their food. There are always lots of people walking on the streets around Amina's house.

As the eldest of her sisters and cousins, Amina is the best at making the peanut sauce that adorns their rice. She has mastered the recipe but often simply sits on a chair in the kitchen, ordering her little sister to crush the peanuts in a certain way or add a bit of this or that. She does the same ordering around for cleaning and other chores.

It has never bothered Amina when people call her bossy, because she knows it's true. Amina had to stop going to school when she was eight years old to help take care of her cousins at home. In spite of that, Amina believed she knew the answer to everything.

Last spring, Amina started coughing. For many weeks, she thought it was a cold because she often developed a cold in the springtime. Slowly spring turned into summer. As everyone waited for the rains to come again, Amina kept coughing. One morning, Amina coughed so hard she coughed up blood, but it was only enough blood to cover her bottom lip. It only happened once, so she tried to ignore the cough. But when the next morning she coughed up more blood, Amina knew it was time to tell her mother that something was wrong.

Amina's mother was worried, but she was almost certain she knew what had been making her daughter so sick for so long. "*Amina, je pense que tu as la tuberculose,*" she told her daughter. "I think you have tuberculosis."

Amina had to admit she didn't know much about tuberculosis. Although she always had all the answers, this time she knew she was in a predicament she couldn't get out of on her own. Amina's mother had overheard the doctors and nurses having conversations about the many people who had tuberculosis during the years she had worked at the hospital. Amina listened nervously as her mother explained that, if she had tuberculosis, she would have to keep away from other people and take antibiotics for many months.

But first, Amina had to be seen by someone at the hospital. Early the next morning, Amina and her aunt got in line to wait to see a doctor or a nurse. First they talked to a nurse. The nurse listened to Amina, who gave them a pass to wait in another line to see the nurse at the lung clinic.

The line at the lung clinic was long; there were many people with the same symptoms as Amina. They waited for a very long time before seeing another nurse. She explained to Amina and her aunt what was going to happen.

"Your symptoms sound very much like tuberculosis. You have been coughing for several weeks, and now you are coughing up some blood. You have had fevers and you have lost weight. I will collect some of what you are coughing up in a jar, and we will send the jar to the laboratory to be examined. But we will assume for now that you do have tuberculosis. You will have to take antibiotics for the next six months, and you will have to come to this clinic five times a week to take them. Do you understand?"

Amina was overwhelmed. She thought about how excited she had been to take the bus to Dakar, the capital city, to visit a friend. Now she could not travel until she finished her treatment. Oddly, she now felt alone sitting next to her favorite aunt. She looked at her aunt, who nodded. "Yes, I understand," Amina said. The nurse explained to Amina that she was lucky to live so close to the hospital, as she wouldn't have to walk very far every day. Amina didn't feel lucky.

Within minutes, Amina had spat into the plastic jar the nurse had provided. Her yellow sputum would go to the laboratory and be grown in a culture over weeks, just as if it had been growing inside her chest. The culture would then be tested for tuberculosis, and she would know for certain if her cough was being caused by tuberculosis. They would not wait for the results to start the treatment, however. She swallowed all the pills she was given, and before she even realized what had happened, Amina and her aunt were back outside the hospital.

Amina walked home in a daze. Now that the nurse had told her she was sick, Amina felt sicker than ever. She was also worried about her family. The nurse had said that if she was in close contact with others, she could easily infect them. What about her sisters and cousins? Could she make them sick? She also tried to think of how she'd gotten sick. Except when she went to the market to buy groceries in the morning, Amina spent most of her time at home.

When they sat down to eat their evening meal, there was very little laughing at the dinner table. Amina's mom was accustomed to seeing sick patients, so she gave her daughter a big hug. The younger girls, though, kept their distance. They were afraid of Amina, which made her feel miserable. Normally, she would have done anything to be away from her cousins. Now when she wanted them close by, they were staying as far away as possible.

The bedrooms were rearranged so that Amina could sleep alone. That meant that Amina's mother would sleep with her two younger sisters. Amina felt very lonely. She'd never slept alone before. Amina pulled on her cousin's hair and made sure to take her younger sister's favorite pillow in to the bedroom with her. She still didn't feel any better. Suddenly, she was very, very sorry that she had been so bossy to everyone. Now when she felt a coughing fit come on, she went in to her bedroom to keep everyone from getting sick.

The first few mornings, Amina felt very nervous before going to the hospital to take her medicines. She'd never taken many medicines before, and she didn't know how she'd feel. But after the second week, Amina was feeling much better. She'd stopped coughing, and her fevers were gone.

When Amina told the nurse how much better she felt, she was surprised at the nurse's stern reaction. "It doesn't matter how good you feel. You need to show up here five mornings a week just like you did when you felt sick. There are still lots of tuberculosis bacteria living inside you, and if you stop taking your medicines they will grow back!"

Amina understood the danger, and she kept taking her medicines. After two months her test results came back and confirmed that Amina had tuberculosis. She was taking the right combination of antibiotics and would just have to keep taking them to be fully healed.

Soon she stopped being afraid of the tuberculosis clinic. She didn't have to be afraid because she knew everyone there. In the mornings Amina would walk the few blocks to the clinic, take her medicines, and walk home. Several other patients also went to the clinic in the mornings to take their medicines. They were mostly older than Amina and came from all over the city to take their medicines. Everyone would smile, swallow their pills, and head home to rest.

Since she was no longer coughing, Amina could no longer infect people around her with tuberculosis. After reassurance from the nurse, Amina was slowly allowed to spend more time with her sisters and cousins. To show how happy she was, Amina took extra care and washed her sister's pillow for her. Amina realized that the pillow wasn't much of a gift, since she had taken it from her sister. So she went down to the market and got her sister a *bin bin*, a long elastic necklace of beads worn low on the waist. Actually, she bought a bunch of *bins bins* that her sisters, her cousins, her aunt, and her mother could choose from.

Finally, after six months of taking antibiotics, Amina was cured of her tuberculosis. She had stopped coughing, and the lab could no longer grow tuberculosis from her cough. She would still have to return to the clinic every few months for checkups, but Amina was back to being a healthy fifteen-year-old. She began sleeping in the same room as her sisters again, and she was more gracious about their sleeping arrangements. She was happy to get to gossip again at night. Amina stopped bossing her family around because she'd come to realize just how much they meant to her.

Part 6

EUROPE

29

The Birthday House

Mary Carleen Veal

"The Birthday House" describes Gabi's struggle with HIV and coinfection with tuberculosis as a young girl in Romania. In the late 1980s, many individuals in Eastern Europe were infected with HIV due to contaminated blood supply. It is important for youth to understand that HIV infection can be spread not only by unprotected sex but also by needles, contaminated blood, and breast milk. Often people become sick because their immune systems are weakened by AIDS. Most people with HIV and AIDS die of sicknesses like pneumonia, malaria, and tuberculosis.

Each time she passed the shop window, Mariana stared at the tiny dollhouse, as if by looking at it long enough, she could make it real. There was something special about the house, something that made Mariana think of magic. She felt she could either become terribly small, which would enable her to open the little brown door and walk inside, or the house could suddenly grow to an immense size, and she could simply move in!

The house was gray plaster, made to look like stone, with pink-trimmed, old-fashioned windows. Painted green vines surrounded the entranceway, and draped cozily over the many windows. Sitting on its little wooden pedestal, the house seemed to be perched on an island of pebbles, rocks, and bushes—a world away from the bustling universe outside the shop window and the endless, colorless rows of massive concrete apartment buildings of Bucharest, Romania.

The first time Mariana saw the house, she asked, "Please, Mami, please, for my birthday?" They were carrying their heavy bags of food to the tram that would take them home, and Mariana's mother did not stop to ask the price. She was tired after her job cleaning offices, and she knew that Mariana's father would be home soon from the factory where he worked, ready for his dinner.

As they rode home, her mother carefully explained, "We have so little money, and you know we must be practical even with birthday gifts. You need a new pullover and new slippers, and your sister had to have extra medicines this month."

Mariana didn't want to have a practical new pullover. She wanted to have the pretty house, so that her imagination would have a place to live and grow. But she understood that her seventeen-year-old sister, Gabi, had to come first. It had always been this way.

Mariana's mother had finally explained the situation last year, when she thought Mariana was old enough to understand and keep the family's secret. Like thousands of other children, Gabi had been infected with HIV, the virus that causes AIDS. This happened because of terrible medical accidents a long time ago when a man named Ceauşescu had been the dictator of Romania. Mariana had been told about some of the bad things the dictator had done in her history class, but this was one thing that was never talked about.

Mariana had been angry, angry because this medical accident had made her sister sick and angry because her parents had not told her the truth before. After all, Mariana was nine now, and she had been able to keep secrets for years—or would be able to, if only people would tell them to her. But she also understood how important this secret was and just how afraid all their neighbors and friends would be of Gabi's illness.

Mariana loved her sister because she was so brave. Sometimes Gabi had to go to the hospital for weeks at a time, and the nurses put needles into her arm when they had to give her injections and IV fluids. Gabi had to take huge pills every day to try to stay well. Mariana did not understand how she could swallow so many. And sometimes the pills that were supposed to make her well made her sick too.

When they arrived home late that afternoon, Mariana tried to tell her sister about the magical house, but Gabi had little energy for conversation. She was lying on the sofa, very tired out from her long day at a technical high school, where she was learning to be a seamstress.

"It sounds pretty, and I will go with you to look at it another day when I feel better," Gabi promised. Gabi was watching her soap opera on TV, the one in Spanish with the Romanian subtitles, that Mariana thought was so boring. But the stories made Gabi feel better. Mariana considered that perhaps watching that soap opera world was like looking in the windows of the little plaster house she had just seen, imagining what it would be like to live there. When Gabi watched those pretty people on TV leading rich, healthy lives, maybe she imagined what it would be like to live that way.

"I will bring you a cool cloth for your head," Mariana offered, and Gabi smiled. It wasn't the cool cloth that would feel so good to her. It was that Mariana would sit beside her, even though she didn't like the television show.

Gabi kept her promise. The next Saturday, she took the tram with Mariana to help with the shopping. That way Mami could stay home and do the family laundry. Since they had no washing machine, this was a very hard job. The girls teased their mother that it would make her strong, like going to a gym. But when they saw their mother bending over the bathtub, scrubbing the muddy jeans, it didn't look at all like those places they saw on TV where people made muscles.

The girls often laughed together when they watched American movies where they saw people who drove home from work, put on special shoes, and then took a walk for exercise. Why didn't they just walk to work, or walk to their buses, or walk with their groceries? Why did they wear funny clothes to walk and carry weights in their hands?

Gabi admired the special house. She even went into the shop and asked the price, while Mariana waited outside. All she said when she came out was, "Let's go get a pastry before we do the shopping." Mariana couldn't bring herself to ask her sister what the house cost. After they finished their treats, they went to the big open market to buy their potatoes, carrots, onions, and apples. Mariana found herself wishing that these things that tasted so good were not so heavy to carry.

Then they decided to go the park. They, like many Romanians living in the big city in small apartments, liked the chance to get outside on the weekends, especially if the weather was nice. On the way, they stopped at the Orthodox church to light candles. Taking out her silver *lei* coins, Gabi bought two candles for each of them.

"We can light one for Grandmother, who has not been feeling well," she explained, "and one for my friend Adriana." Adriana had been one of Gabi's friends in the hospital who had died a month ago. Not only did Adriana have AIDS; she also had had tuberculosis, or TB. When she then got measles, she died very quickly.

Both the girls knew several people with TB who did not have AIDS. TB was something that people got when they were poor. Their own grandmother, who lived in a village, had TB a few years ago; so did some of her neighbors, including their young cousin Alex. Gabi could remember her grandmother complaining that she couldn't get the medicine she needed. Things were better under the old dictator, during communist times, her grandmother would say. At least then, old people knew they could get an aspirin when they needed it.

Their *bunica* (grandmother) was a funny lady, but since she lived in the country, she lived a very different life than the girls did in Bucharest. In the summer, when Gabi was well enough, the girls would go to stay with her in the tiny village where there were more carts and horses than cars. There were only three stations on the television, and the toilet was outside in the yard.

They liked working in their grandmother's garden, feeding the chickens, and playing with her dog. In Bucharest, their only dogs were the street dogs that belonged to no one, although some people left their bones and scraps out for them where the garbage was kept. They were friendly enough, but it was not the same as being able to run on the mountain paths with Bunica's big white farm dog, Albui.

The city park was crowded, despite the fact that the day was cold and damp. The snow had melted, but cold rain had followed, making the ground very muddy. Mariana tried to think about summer, to concentrate on going to the little farm near the mountains. Imagination was such a good friend, she thought, except, of course, when she got into trouble for daydreaming in school!

While she and Gabi walked by the lake at the park, trying to step around the worst of the mud puddles, her sister asked, "Why do you like that little house so much? What would you do with it?"

"I would look at it and wish we lived there," Mariana answered as she put her arm around her sister's waist. "I can see all the special rooms that would be inside, lots of rooms, so that Mami and Tata wouldn't have to sleep in the living room, and Mami would have a washing machine. You could have a big soft bed in your own room. We could even have a cat then, to chase away a mouse in our house."

She had Gabi laughing then. Mariana loved it when Gabi laughed; her pain faded away into her giggles and grins.

Taking a seat on a park bench, the girls talked about her birthday, about the creamy *tort*, a special cake she wanted, like the one in the pastry shop window, with colorful pieces of fruit on top. She only had to wait until next Saturday!

Each morning at school during the week, she thought only of her birthday, wishing again, then wishing some more, that she would not just get a pullover or slippers. The mornings in school seemed extra long; Mariana was extra hungry, too. Because the schools in Bucharest were so crowded, the students had to come in two shifts. Younger ones like Mariana had classes early in the morning, while older ones like Gabi went in the afternoon. Romanian schools didn't have lunchrooms like

Mariana had seen in American movies. They didn't even have lunches, just some milk and bread for the younger students during their short break. By the time she got home she was always very hungry for a big, big sandwich and hot soup, if some was left from the night before.

Gabi ate before she went to school, because it would be dark when she came home again. It was hard for her to take her special medicines and have something to eat at the right time when she took her pills, because she was so afraid that her friends would see her and ask questions. She knew that other people would be terrified of her having HIV and that someone might find a way to have her dismissed from school if they knew her secret.

But the days did pass until the week at school was finally done, and Mariana even had the good news that she made a 10, the perfect grade, on her history test! This test had been a difficult one, about the days when the Romans had ruled Romania so many centuries ago. She liked knowing the rich history of her country and longed for the day when she and Gabi could go to the Black Sea. She not only wanted to see the ocean but also the ancient Roman ruins. Someday, Tata promised, someday.

Her long-awaited Saturday and her birthday cake did finally arrive. Several gift bags were placed beside the cake. She opened each bag in turn and had almost given up hope. Then, at last, Gabi came close, with hands held behind her back. She gave her little sister the traditional kiss on each cheek. "*La multi ani*, Mariana!" she said, handing her a beautiful flowered bag. Mariana waited a long moment before opening it; inside lay the small house, as perfect as she remembered.

Mariana lay in bed that night, her birthday house nestled in the blanket beside her, looking at every detail. She decided that her room would be the one behind the upstairs window on the right. Mariana could see into that room, imagining sunny yellow walls and a big bed filled with soft, cuddly teddy bears. She decided that she would ask her mother for old magazines, and then cut out pictures of rooms and furniture. She would make a special book of her own, about how she would decorate the inside of her house.

Mariana knew she would give the nicest bedroom to Gabi, because Gabi had to stay in bed sometimes when she didn't feel well. She could see that special pink room, Gabi's favorite color. It would be at the back of her house, where the painted plaster formed a small balcony. Gabi could feed birds from the balcony, and they could put out pots of bright red geraniums in the summer sun.

It was hard to slow her busy, excited mind down to even think about sleep, but she knew that Mami would come in soon to make sure the light was off. Oh, she wished her house could be real! She wished her family could have a comfortable life, like she saw families have in far-away places. Then maybe, just maybe, if they lived like that, Gabi would feel better and be stronger. That is what Mariana had wished most of all when she blew out the candles on her cake—that Gabi would be well.

Mariana felt her eyes beginning to close. She was tired after her wonderful day. As she snuggled under her blanket, she was happy. It was a beautiful gift to have her birthday house of dreams and to know she could visit anytime she wanted.

30

Little Ashes

Laurie R. Hibbett

"Little Ashes" speaks to the epidemic of youth smoking in France. Smoking is directly responsible for 90 percent of lung cancer cases. Smoking-related diseases claim an estimated 438,000 American lives each year. This number includes many who are affected indirectly—such as victims of secondhand smoke and babies who are exposed to nicotine's carcinogens by prenatal maternal smoking. This narrative provides a platform for students to discuss the risks associated with smoking in the atmosphere of their peers and with the guidance of a teacher.

The *banlieue* neighborhood of Eaubonne lies just northwest of Paris, and you can get there in about fifteen minutes from Gare du Nord. As you pull out of Paris, you see train tracks, abandoned trains, crumbling buildings, high rises, and slums. Eaubonne is a fairly typical neighborhood. It has its fair share of pollution and cheap shops, but it is also blessed with *boulangeries*, *patisseries*, cafés, and most of its houses boast gardens overflowing with rose bushes and other flowers.

But on this gray November afternoon, when the roses had all been trimmed back for the winter, the streets of Eaubonne looked empty and bleak. The front door of 17 Rue Pontoise opened, and a slender, dark-skinned girl stepped out and slammed it behind her, her eyes blazing and pretty lips drawn tight. She had had another fight with her adopted mother. Alienor marched away from the house, away from the place where she felt like a perpetual stranger. Her father had died when she was a young girl, and her distant cousins had adopted her. But Alienor's mother had been African, and her thick dark hair and dark skin set her apart from the pale family who, from the first day of Alienor's arrival at their house, had treated her like an outsider, an inconvenience.

Alienor stormed out the gate and called her best friend, Simone.

"Hey, Simone. I had to get out of the house. Want to go to Lu's?"

"Aw, Alienor. I've got that paper to write! You know that. I can't spend all afternoon—"

"*Come on*, Simone. Please? Just for an hour. Meet me at the corner?"

"Fine, you win. I'll be there in seven minutes."

The girls met at their traditional meeting spot, the edge of a park that was equidistant from each of their houses. They each pulled out a pack of cigarettes. The girls were only sixteen, but Simone had started stealing Camels from her older brother about a year ago. And now that they were sixteen they could sometimes get away with buying cigarettes on their own. Which, increasingly, they did. In fact, what had started out as a cigarette every few days turned quickly into a few cigarettes every day, and, before they realized what was happening, each girl had gotten so chained to the habit that she was smoking almost a pack a day.

Alienor flicked the lighter, cupping her hand over the end of the cigarette to protect it from the November wind. It lit up, and the little red ember had a cheering effect—all of Eaubonne was drenched in gray it seemed, sky, buildings, roads, everything. The little burning end of the cigarette made her feel more alive, somehow. Simone lit hers as well, and the girls inhaled deeply. They each felt better instantly.

Alienor didn't mind that her mother had yelled at her, and Simone forgot about the fact that her father had gotten laid off from his job a few days earlier.

They walked slowly toward Chez Lucie, their favorite café. It was run by Lucie and her husband, Jean-Michelle. (Though everyone called them Lu and Jean-Mi.) Alienor and Simone sat down at the bar and ordered coffee. When Lu brought the tiny white cups over and set them down she paused and gave the girls a concerned look. Lucie was fifty-ish; she had no children of her own but was the informal mother of all the young people who frequented the restaurant. Simone and Alienor were particular favorites.

"What's wrong, Lu?" Alienor asked. "You're not going to start lecturing us about smoking again, are you?"

"No, no." Lu sighed. "You've heard the lecture enough times, I'm sure, and besides, I know from personal experience that all the lectures in the world aren't enough to make someone stop smoking."

Jean-Mi sidled up beside his wife and put an arm around her waist. "But of course," he said, grinning mischievously, "only true love can make someone quit the filthy habit. Lu stopped because of her adoring passion for *me*, her humble, kind, wise, generous, good-looking spouse, right, *mon poussin*?"

Lu laughed. "Don't flatter yourself. You had nothing to do with it. I quit because I didn't want to make my skin wrinkle! Quit for you! What an idea!" Jean-Mi pretended to be hurt by his wife's playful cruelty and walked back to the kitchen whistling "Cold, Cold Heart." The girls laughed but sobered up as Lu continued to muse about wrinkles. "Yes," she sighed, "you see those old women whose mouths are pinched up and whose cheeks sadly creased by smoking. Of course, wrinkles are natural and a true Frenchwoman will accept the signs of age with grace and dignity. Phooey on plastic surgery, I say. But you can tell a woman who's been smoking for twenty or thirty years. The smoke sucks the life right out of your skin." Alienor and Simone exchanged wide-eyed glances of surprise, and Lu continued, pretending not to notice. "But I won't lecture you girls; you know me, I'm not the lecturing sort. You can smoke all you want to. Oh, I need to get back to work. I'll leave you two in peace."

The girls meekly returned to their coffee. The talk about wrinkles had had an effect. Before either one could think of something to say, Lu walked back by and leaned toward them. "And just between us, girls," she said softly, "I *did* quit for Jean-Mi, of course. It was partly about the wrinkles but mostly, well . . . kisses were never meant to taste of smoke. But don't tell him I said that. His insufferable ego is already puffed up." She winked. The girls smiled—they knew that Lu and Jean-Mi loved each other despite their apparent antagonism.

This time Alienor and Simone took solemn sips of their coffee. Alienor decided to change the subject; she didn't want to think about giving up smoking to prevent wrinkles or for the sake of amour. Wrinkles, to her fifteen-year-old mind, seemed a million years away, and she couldn't imagine any sort of love that would require the sacrifice of such an innocuous habit. "So," Alienor began with a sigh, "my mom and I had another fight this afternoon."

"Oh, sweetie, what happened?" Simone asked sympathetically. Her own family had troubles of its own, and she and Alienor constantly took refuge at Lu's to escape the emotional—and sometimes physical—traumas of their respective homes.

"Well, she started listing all these things I'm doing wrong—my grades aren't good enough, I don't keep my room clean enough, I'm disrespectful, irresponsible, and all the usual stuff. So I told her it's hard for me to be respectful when she treats me like I'm the worst thing that's ever happened to her. She hasn't been to one of my basketball games yet this season. She really just doesn't care about me at all! I don't fit in with this family, even after six years of living with them . . ." A few tears welled up in Alienor's dark eyes, but she brushed them away quickly and took a deep breath. She was determined to be strong. Simone was quiet for a moment and pulled out another cigarette.

"Listen, Alienor, I need to tell you something." Simone took a deep breath as she lit her cigarette. "I'm trying to quit smoking. But . . . I can't. Every time I try to stop I start to feel so *hopeless*. There's this creeping feeling of loneliness, and it's almost suffocating at times. I'll tell myself, 'OK, this is it. The last pack, the last cigarette.' And then I'll go for maybe half a day, and it drives me so crazy I feel like I have to find another cigarette or I'll literally die. I haven't told you about it because . . ." She trailed off, took a nervous drag of the cigarette, wondering what her friend would say. Smoking had become such a bond between them; she felt that quitting would betray their friendship in a sense.

"But Simone," Alienor exclaimed, a little shocked, "why do you need to stop? Just save yourself the pain and agony, and keep smoking!" Alienor didn't realize how attached she herself had become; the thought of living without cigarettes was almost incomprehensible. Cigarettes had become the perfect distraction from her discontented life; they provided the perfect escape from her family, the perfect little secret to keep from the world, the perfect accessory to complement her personality. Even as she spoke to Simone she glanced at herself in the large mirror across the restaurant and thought how charming she looked holding the cigarette. No matter that she was having trouble keeping up with the other girls on her basketball team. And all that talk about lung cancer couldn't really be true, and even if it *was* true that was such a long way off. And wrinkles? Bah! Her skin was perfect and always would be. And besides—

"Alienor! You're not even listening to me!" Simone startled her friend out of her reverie. "I was *saying* that there are a lot of reasons I want to stop. This is getting really expensive, for one thing. And Lu's right about the wrinkles, and after seeing my grandfather in the hospital, you know . . ." She tapped the cigarette lightly on the ashtray, and one piece of ash joined the other ashes in the little glass dish.

Alienor nodded. She could, in the end, understand why her friend was having such a hard time. Simone's grandfather had been in the hospital for almost a year with emphysema after a lifetime of smoking. Simone had been deeply affected by seeing him rasping and unable to fill his weakened lungs with air. Every time she left the hospital she promised herself that she wouldn't smoke any more. And usually a few hours later she would crumble and pick up another pack.

"Well, Simone, I'm sorry. I do not know what to tell you. I have no idea how to stop smoking, because I have no desire to stop. You better talk to Lu about it. But I think you should take my advice and save yourself the misery of quitting. I've heard that nicotine withdrawal is pretty much the worst thing in the world."

At that point, Lu walked back over. "You girls want some more coffee?" she asked.

"Sure, Lu," Simone said. Lu picked up their cups and walked over to the espresso machine. When she brought back the tiny cups and set them down she leaned against the bar. "Alright, girls, spill. I can tell something's up. Since when do you keep secrets from Aunt Lu?"

"Well, Lu," Simone began. She almost didn't know how to tell Lucie about wanting to quit, after all these months of cavalierly ignoring the kind lady's gentle admonitions about the dangers of smoking. Besides, she didn't like to admit that she had gotten herself into a situation she couldn't get out of on her own. She took a deep breath. "Lucie, I want to quit smoking. But I can't. Part of me loves it too much. And I go crazy when I try to stop. It's too hard . . ." Simone trailed off, ashed her cigarette again, and took a long drag. Lucie looked at her with wise old eyes; she knew all too well that feeling of wanting to quit but still being so tied to cigarettes that you have to smoke even as you talk about wanting to quit.

"Simone, quitting smoking was the hardest thing I've ever done. I smoked for thirteen years, and by that time I realized that I loved cigarettes more than anything else in my life. Sure, I was worried about the health issues, but I became so afraid that my heart was dying in some ways. I let cigarettes become my best friend. I was so dependent on nicotine that I didn't care to think about the fact that my smoking was destroying my relationship with Jean-Mi. When I woke up in the morning I wouldn't talk to him until I'd had my coffee and a cigarette."

Simone had reached the end of her cigarette and thoughtfully rubbed the burning end in the ashtray, which contained a growing pile of ashes and cigarette butts. She looked carefully at the ashtray and realized how disgusting it was, all those dirty ashes . . .

"Honey, listen," Lucie said, "I don't want to preach about this because I know it doesn't work. But I've been there and I know what it's like. I think you should be brave and keep trying to quit. I'll give you free coffee whenever you come in—and Alienor yours is on me too if you can keep away from cigarettes while you're in here. Simone, it'll be hard. I'm not going to lie to you. It will hurt, and you'll have moments when you want to curl up and cry forever. Listen, keep thinking about it. It takes time to make up your mind, but I can see in your eyes that you truly do no not want to be chained to smoking anymore. That's the biggest part, because most people just let the nicotine lie to them for their whole lives. That's what addiction does, girls." Lucie picked up the ashtray, dumped out the ashes, and rinsed it out. She replaced the clean glass bowl, and looked at Simone and Alienor. "Please come back soon if you want to talk some more. You'll need some help, and you know I'm always here for you two." Lucie knew that the girls each had enough trouble at home and needed a sympathetic, motherly ear. She sighed as the girls took their last sips of coffee and walked back out into the cold November twilight.

31

Broken Strings

The ArtReach Foundation

"Broken Strings" tells the story of Amra's family during the war in Bosnia and Herzegovina, commonly known as the Bosnian War, an international armed conflict that took place between March 1992 and November 1995. This war had several sides, but Muslims were targeted and suffered greatly. This narrative highlights the health problems induced by war in addition to showing the ways in which mental health is affected by conflict.

Amra and Ivana sat anxiously waiting for the final school bell to ring. They eagerly awaited the chance to run down the crooked cobblestone streets past the bakery, where the scents of fresh baked sweets would fill their nostrils. They looked forward to seeing families walking together in the streets, smiling and waving at neighbors. There was a certain air of peace and civility among the people in the streets. Once free of the crowded street, the girls would join hands and skip the rest of the way to the city park. They would sing a familiar tune from their childhood as they passed the old church and finish the song as they rounded the last corner into the shadow of the tower looming over the mosque on the edge of the park.

The park was their hideout. It was also the place where they had first met a few years before. Since that day, the girls have never been apart. Amra and Ivana did everything together; they went to the same school, sat at the same desk, took ballet together, and studied together. They lived two blocks away from each other and often slept over at each other's houses: one day at Amra's, the next at Ivana's. Over the years, the families had found a common kinship in each other and often spent evenings together and had even vacationed together on the coast the previous summer. The strong bond forged between these two families allowed Amra and Ivana to feel like sisters. Nothing could separate them.

When the girls left the park, Amra hurried Ivana home, eager to show her the wonderful surprise she had received for her birthday. Her parents had presented her with a big box, and inside it she had found something incredible, something she had wanted for a long time and had begged her parents to give her. They always had some excuse: it was too late to go shopping, they would make time during the following weekend, or, simply, it was too expensive. But there it was. Her eyes had bulged, and she had smiled so big her mouth hurt. She had slowly moved her hand into the deep box and touched the fine wood. "Finally," she had said as she picked up the beautiful, new, shiny red violin.

The girls finally reached Amra's home; they greeted her mother and ran off toward Amra's bedroom. Amra picked up her red violin to show Ivana. Ivana's eyes lit up when she saw the violin. Ivana had begun learning to play the piano and Ivana's father, a music teacher, had promised to teach Amra to play the violin once she had got one. They had decided that they would become a famous duo and perform all around Europe. "We can now have our duet!" she said to Amra. Amra smiled and placed the red violin on her dresser.

Amra couldn't sleep that night. She had curled up under her blankets in the perfect position to gaze at her new red violin. Just as Amra had fallen asleep, she heard a sharp noise outside her window. The apartment shook. Pictures and dishes fell to floor. Amra jumped from her bed and ran to her door to find her mother. She could hear yelling and screaming outside her window and louder explosions that sounded like firecrackers. The firecrackers didn't stop. She started to shake with fear. At that moment, her mother burst open the door and grabbed her. She held Amra for a solid moment, and then Amra looked into her mother's eyes and saw fear.

Her mother spoke calmly, "Come now, my love, we must hurry to the basement." She took Amra by the wrist—her little brother was already gently pressed against her chest—and hurried the two of them out of the apartment and down the stairs to the basement. They sat together in a small huddle, comforting each other at each loud firecracker. Amra buried her face in her mother's chest as she heard the roar of the firecrackers outside.

The basement was dark with only four small windows close to the ceiling and no carpet. The concrete was cold on Amra's bare feet. She held hands with her mother and brother, shivering as she looked around the tiny room. Amra's neighbors were there; babies cried and mothers comforted them. Amra heard one young mother tell her toddler, "You must remain quiet or they will come and take you away."

What is going on? Amra thought to herself. *Where is Papa?*

Amra listened as the woman to her right cried quietly, and the woman across the room whispered, "There were many people killed . . . many taken away." The woman next to her gasped, "They did not even spare the children."

Amra turned toward her mother for comfort and clenched her fist. *Who is "they"?* Amra thought to herself. *What did the woman mean, people were killed? Who would do this?*

Confusion and fear gripped the women and children huddled in the basement. The shouting from outside drew closer and they heard the sound of men's footsteps coming down the stairs. As the footsteps became louder, the women clutched their children tighter. Amra's mother took her two children and covered their heads with her arms. She pulled them in tight and kissed each one on the head. "I love you so much," Amra's mother whispered softly into her ear.

The footsteps stopped outside the door to the basement: there was a moment of silence. Then, *BANG!*

The sound of cold steel on the outside of the door echoed through the basement.

BANG! The door slammed and shook. *BANG, BANG, BANG!*

Unhinged, the door flew open. Big men swept in one at a time and began grabbing people at random. They used their rifles as clubs to beat at the kneeling mass of bodies. Amra pressed closer to her mother. She grabbed her brother's hand and looked him in the eyes: his eyes were red with tears. She shut her eyes tightly and sobbed.

"Where are the men?" the soldiers shouted angrily. Amra lifted her eyes over her mother's arm for an instant and saw a soldier grab her neighbor by the hair and drag her screaming across the room. Another pressed the barrel of his rifle hard against a woman's face. The woman grimaced in pain. They shouted again, "Where are the men?" Amra closed her eyes. Everyone was screaming, the explosions from outside were deafening, and all Amra could hear was the beat of her mother's heart. The men began dragging several women out of the room, their children still clutching to their limbs. Amra opened her eyes just long enough to see the soldiers kicking the children off their mothers. Amra cried harder.

And then, they left as quickly as they had come. Silence.

Amra opened her eyes hoping that this was a nightmare and that she would soon wake up. She imagined herself tucked under her blankets in bed, ready for her birthday. She knew, however, that the cold cement floor beneath her was not her bed. She looked around the room and saw blank stares of the remaining women. The room was filling with daylight, and Amra saw the mothers covered in blood mixed with tears. A five-year-old girl began to cry, but her mother had been carried off by the soldiers, and she was alone. An older woman crawled to the girl, took her into her arms, and tried to comfort her.

The women and children remained in the basement throughout the day, listening to the horrific sounds outside their windows. The firecrackers had not ceased, and there was no sign that they would stop. They sat in silence and disbelief. They listened. One woman sat with her knees in her hands, repeating, "How could this happen? How could this happen?" Amra lay next to her mother, frightened. She envisioned her friends coming over for her party. How would they know to come to the basement? Would the soldiers let them in? Amra rested her head on her mother's thigh as she thought of Ivana.

"Momma," Amra asked, "do you think Ivana is OK?" Her mother pursed her lips and said nothing.

"What about Papa, where is Papa?" Amra pleaded. Her mother lowered her sad eyes to Amra and said, "I do not know, my love, I do not know."

"Momma, what is happening? Why did those men take those women? Why were they so angry?" Amra began to cry again.

"My love, you must not trouble yourself with so many questions. Quiet."

"But what if the men took Ivana away?" Amra cried out.

"You should tell her," a woman from the corner whispered to Amra's mother. Amra's mother closed her eyes, inhaled a deep breath, and leaned back against the concrete.

Amra closed her eyes and tried to sleep; she tried to force herself into a dream about performing with her new violin with Ivana. The night was difficult. When Amra awoke next to her brother, she was covered in the blanket from her bed. She looked up at her mother's tired face as she offered Amra a piece of bread with jam. During the night her mother had snuck upstairs to their apartment. Now the sun was rising through the small windows. Amra looked around the dimly lit room and could see that some of the women had left during the night and had not returned.

"I want to go home, Momma," Amra whispered.

"There is nothing to go back to," she replied. Amra had never seen her mother's face so stern before.

"What about my room, my violin?" Amra pleaded; she felt desperate.

"Your violin is fine, baby, right where you left it." Her mother did not have the courage to tell Amra the soldiers had ransacked their apartment, breaking everything they could, destroying photos and precious keepsakes, overturning furniture and tearing clothes. Even Amra's beautiful violin had been destroyed.

"I hope Ivana is OK," Amra said gazing into her mother's eyes. Amra's mother swallowed hard, gathering her strength, and wiped the hair from her daughter's eyes.

"Ivana is OK, Amra. She left the night before last. When she left you she went home and her father took the family away."

Amra was relieved but gave her mother an innocent look of confusion.

"Ivana is a Serb. Her family is of Serbian descent. Those men, the soldiers that came in yesterday are Serbs." Her mother's eyes began to fill with tears. "They do not like us because we are Muslim. They want us all gone."

"But . . . Ivana . . . is my sister. Her father was going to teach . . ."

"Her father was one of those men yesterday," Amra's mother interrupted. Amra looked up at her mother in disbelief, shaking her head "no."

"Amra, look at me." She looked past the tears into her mother's face. Her mother had a cold, hard, serious expression that was foreign to Amra. "We must never speak of Ivana again. We are no longer family."

Amra looked down at the blanket she was wrapped in and wept as her mother held her tight against her chest. Her mother sang her to sleep with the lullaby they sang together each night; the hours passed, and there was no relief.

The next day brought more of the same. The Serbs destroyed the town, house by house, killing each Muslim they found. They spared no one: women, children, elderly. Those who died quickly were considered lucky. Others were carried off behind buildings by groups of men, and their cries for help haunted those that had gathered in the shelter. They were helpless. Days passed, and the group continued to huddle together. Patience.

Amra's dreams were full of her town. She stood in the center square and waved to neighbors, classmates, and friends. But, even in her dreams, the dark reality pierced through. "Are you a Serb," she asked. "A Muslim?" Everyone looked the same as they did before they escaped to the basement. The same dark features: same dark hair, dark eyes, and smile. She tried to determine who was a Serb and who was a Muslim. She couldn't: they all looked the same.

She awoke from her dream to her mother shaking her softly. "Everything is going to be alright," she said. "The men have returned to save us. Your father is coming. He will take us to safety." She sobbed and put her head in her hands. "We are going home."

The night witnessed a heroic struggle by her father and others who fought for the safety of the Muslims. By daybreak, the last of the Serb soldiers had left for the hills and the town was free. Slowly, Amra and her family joined the others who had found relief in the shelters as they emerged into the daylight. The firecrackers were silent and the sun was warm. At last, Amra would be able to go home, and she would be able to hug her father and play her beautiful violin.

Amra grabbed for the tattered doorknob to their apartment, but the door was no longer attached. Amra's eyes bulged as she saw the clothes, books, and torn photos scattered across the living room floor. Everything was ruined. Amra raced down the hallway to her room, fearful of what she might find. She stopped. Before her lay the broken red violin. She knelt down and ran her fingers over the broken instrument. She picked up the broken strings that had once made a beautiful sound. Determined, she weaved the strings back through the pegs and tightened them carefully, holding the broken violin together. She found the crooked bow underneath her bed and drew it across the strings. The violin whined and gasped trying to come back to life.

"We will fix it," her mother unquestionably stated.

Amra and her mother cleaned the apartment together, piecing together what they could salvage from the destruction. After Amra finally fell asleep, her father returned. Amra's mother rushed to the door at the sounds of the familiar footsteps approaching. From the darkness he entered the apartment and collapsed into her embrace.

Life did not return to normal for Amra's family. The town had been liberated, but the Serbs had only retreated as far as the hills that surrounded the town. Often grenades and bombs would go off in the town, forcing people to flee at a moment's notice. Snipers aimed their rifles and shot passersby. Amra watched as her father bravely pulled a boy from the street into the safe confines of their building.

As each day passed, Amra became more accustomed to her new life. She learned how to travel quietly and safety, when to cross the streets, and when to find shelter. She grew accustomed to spending nights in the shelter with other families, never being safe or having enough food. She knew deep down that survival was all that mattered.

Many nights, Amra dreamed of playing her violin with Ivana on the piano. She missed Ivana and didn't understand why they were so different. Why the soldiers had tried to kill her family, but Ivana's had escaped. Amra knew that she could not ask her parents these questions. She knew that her dreams were simply dreams. Her violin would not be fixed, and she certainly would not get a new one. Her mother suffered enough trying to figure out how to pay for food.

Months passed, and life remained a struggle. One morning as the fog lifted, the hills fell silent, and Amra's neighbors cautiously stepped outside to see the thundering rattle of the white military vehicles with "U.N." painted on the hoods. A tall man dressed in a military uniform, speaking a language Amra could not understand stepped from the first vehicle. Her father spoke with the uniformed man for a few minutes, courageously shaking his hand and welcoming him into their home for coffee.

"These men are from the United Nations," he whispered excitedly to Amra as he grabbed her hand and shuffled into the apartment. He turned to the crowd and said, "They are from the United Nations. They are here to protect us."

The elderly began to weep but little was said.

The military vehicles were followed by trucks filled with food, medicine, and blankets. Most importantly, the U.N. workers brought news. Amra heard the conversations between townspeople and the U.N.

workers and was astonished by the news: your country is at war.

Within weeks the town was flooded with strangers seeking safety from the war with the Serbs. The U.N. workers called them refugees. Everyone seemed to have lost someone in their family. "Have you seen my son Damir?" one woman asked holding the photo of a handsome boy, sixteen years of age.

"My husband, Ismet, has been missing for weeks. Do you have any news?"

"Edis, is Edis here?"

"What about Armin, or his brother Elvis?"

The lists grew, and more photos were pinned up in the center of town.

Months after the terrible first night in the shelter, it was announced that the school would reopen. Reluctantly the parents walked their children up the crooked cobblestone streets to the schoolhouse. In the beginning, many fathers remained outside the school and waited all day for their children to finish. The first day, Amra was assigned a desk on the third row, next to the window. She did not know any of the other girls who sat with her, but it didn't matter. She looked out and saw the ruins of the old mosque and beyond it, the park. She dreamed of a time when she might see Ivana again, of what they would say to each other.

The building shook, and a deafening roar sent the students diving for the safety beneath their desks. Some children cried, but most of the students sat and listened. The jets roared through the clouds in the sky, and on the distant hillside, there was a tremendous explosion. That day, Amra accepted that this war would never end. She stopped dreaming.

However, the war did end. The fighting stopped, but nobody believed it, no Muslim felt safe in Bosnia at that time. Even though the foreign soldiers remained, and the Serbs did not return, everyone waited in fear.

Today, Amra still looks through the window of her school trying to make sense of this horrific experience, but she still cannot understand the horrific things she saw, and she cannot forget the pain from her mother's face. She cannot understand why her Serbian neighbors turned against them. She cannot understand the violence that resulted because of her religion and heritage.

Now in high school, Amra attends class without fear or the anxiety that came with the knowledge that she might have to run to the shelter at a moment's notice. She has new friends and is grateful to still have her family. Many of her friends lost their fathers during the war. Some of them lost both parents and now they live with their grandparents. Although Amra has lost Ivana, she will never forget their dreams of making music together.

For many months, Amra mourned the loss of her shiny red violin. Because she had no money to repair it, Amra gave her violin to her music teacher at school. Her music classroom was nothing more than a blackboard shattered with bullets. Over the next few months, Amra and her teacher rebuilt the violin, string by string. Once the strings were taut and the body was repaired, Amra devoted hours to practicing her violin and advancing her knowledge of music.

Today, Amra plays her red violin in the Sarajevo orchestra. She still hopes to play a duet with Ivana someday.

32

Envisioning Invisibility

Athena Stevens

"Envisioning Invisibility" follows the path of two sisters in London, England. It aims to increase awareness of body image and the functionality of our bodies in addition to increasing awareness of cerebral palsy (CP) and other physical disabilities. This narrative also explores ways in which people perceive their own bodies and the ways they think that society perceives them.

It was high summer on Tottenham Court Road, and floods of people were exiting the London underground station to escape the stuffy subways down below. The station was an incredible capsule that held people from all walks of life together. Here the African sits next to the young Japanese woman, who sits next to the Colombian, who sits next to the Indian, who sits next to the agnostic, who sits next to the Swedish father of three, who stands next to the Persian. And although this diverse city is far from perfect, it is, for the most part, peaceful.

Samantha and Ginny were not traveling on the underground that day. In fact Ginny has never been on the underground because it is too difficult and fatiguing for her to use the subway system, or the tube as they call it in London, with her CP. In London, the capital of the world, there are steps everywhere. Only one in four hundred babies is born with CP in the UK, but many other people suffer from disabilities that make negotiating steps an impossibility, and downtown London is therefore inaccessible to all of them as well.

Ginny was born with CP, a brain injury that results from lack of oxygen before, during, or shortly after birth. It affected every detail of Ginny's life except her mind. Most people who met Ginny assumed that she was slow or even stupid. But Ginny was always thinking. She was thinking about which way she should lean to keep her wheelchair from tipping over. She thought about exactly what to wear that day so it would be easy for Samantha to help her try on clothes. She thought about which store would be the least crowded at this hour so Samantha wouldn't find this outing too stressful. Ginny knew she was lucky. CP came in all sorts of forms, but hers was considered mild. Still, she could not walk, feed herself, or even comb her own hair. Her sister helped her with all of these things each morning.

Ginny and her sister traveled downtown from their house in Hounslow East by taking three wheelchair-accessible buses and walking a quarter of a mile past all of the homes in Notting Hill. It took the girls two very difficult hours, more than twice the time it would have taken on the tube. This, however, was a rare day, as each one of the bus divers was good enough to put the ramp down so that Ginny could get on the bus. Often the bus drivers would refuse to make eye contact with the girls, or else they would claim that the ramp was broken so that they wouldn't have to take the time to put it down. Today, however, the drivers must have known it was Ginny's birthday.

Samantha is older than Ginny, and she knows that many people are staring at her and her sister. Samantha wishes that they both could disappear into air. Unlike Ginny with her rubber tires and metal chair frame, Samantha is doing a much better job of being invisible. "Are you hungry?" she asks, bending over to talk into her sister's ear above the roar of the London high street.

Ginny waits outside of the café while her sister runs in to get lunch, because there are steps to get in. Every kind of person you can imagine walks by the coffee shop on that busy street in London and still Ginny feels alone. She doesn't look like anyone else on this street. The fashion stores, the women with bags rushing here and there, even the vendors stand on two legs and flash their perfectly straight seams. This city may be where everyone else feels at home, but even a major café chain cannot welcome her from off the street. Samantha comes back with a sandwich, a chocolate muffin, and some tea for Ginny and just an espresso for herself.

"I thought you were getting yourself lunch as well," Ginny says. Ginny knows that her sister hasn't been hungry for a while. She did not eat breakfast and only had an apple the night before. She wonders why her sister's appetite has become so meager. But the answer is simple. Samantha hates how people stare at her almost as much as she hates how they stare at Ginny. Samantha has learned about a condition called anorexia, a condition that leads someone to try to control his or her weight by not eating. But Samantha would never do that. Not eating would lead to painful illnesses and bone problems, among a thousand other things. Samantha would never do anything to jeopardize her health. She has seen what health problems have done to her sister. She would never become anorexic. But she just can't eat. And what is as hard to swallow is how badly both girls feel the need to disappear simply because they don't have the same pace and rhythm as everyone else seems to in their city. And so as Ginny eats the sandwich that her sister holds, they watch the people walk by on the busiest street in the world with their bags and their coffees, hopping on and off of curbs and stairs—going places and eating things that both girls feel are forbidden to them.

Most people don't realize the connection between these two sisters. Yes, they share the same family as well as everything in their lives. They share the same room in the same semidetached home that is exactly like every other house in that neighborhood. But unlike the houses on the street, these girls feel out of place all the time. Always out of place, going up the down staircase—they just feel like they can never fit in anywhere, even on their birthdays.

"Can we go to H&M first?" The hip and young clothing chain is Ginny's favorite even though it can be a madhouse in the afternoon. The clothes flung down on the floor by careless customers, the accessible changing room which is always full of trash, and the maddening women trying to get somewhere in the store all contribute to the overall feeling of rush and inconvenience.

"Nothing fits me right there. You know that."

"It's still the morning; no one will be there yet. We'll just look around. Please, it's my birthday. I want to shop where everyone else does."

Samantha says nothing and looks at her half-full coffee cup, debating whether or not to drink the entire thing. She is tired on this warm day. And, as always, she wants more. She wants more coffee, more food, more accessible subway stations, more people willing to help her and her sister on a day out. She is in one of the most remarkable cities in the world and she wants more.

"Alright, let's go. But don't be surprised if I get in a bad mood because the music is loud," Samantha teases as she shoots a smile to her sister. Samantha jumps behind Ginny's chair and pushes it with gleeful force. They are careful to avoid every crack in the very uneven sidewalk. Failure to do so could result in a fall and complete embarrassment. Although the girls face different physical challenges, they share a deep friendship; they each love the other for who she is inside and out.

Postscript

Emily Mendenhall

We hope that the preceding stories have provoked much debate in your classrooms, stimulated conversations during school lunches, and filled dinner tables with story retelling. Just as John Snow initiated the field of public health by identifying the polluted Broad Street pump as the source of the cholera epidemic, we too can all become public health practitioners. This particular compilation of stories is the product of many collective years of work in public health and activism, but at the center of each narrative is the author's dedication to effecting social change on a small scale in her or his community. *Our most important goal is to convey that you have the power to improve the world by the choices you make.*

The stories in this book describe the complexity of public health situations that affect individuals, communities, and the world. "Toshio and the Crane," "Broken Strings," and "The Birthday House" demonstrate that history and politics can influence health. However, as we see in "A Brighter Future," "Paola's Tijuana," "The Pen Pals," "Joey and the Rain," "Growing Up Maya," and "Rosa's Farm," health risks are sometimes less visible because they can result from problems associated with violence, migration, oppression, and pollution. "*Maji Ni Uhai*," "The Shaman's Daughter," and "Karai Guasu's Cock-a-Doodle-Doo" illustrate the importance of safe water for keeping people and communities healthy. Public health, however, also aims to prevent disease. Infectious diseases such as tuberculosis, malaria, and HIV/AIDS have high mortality and morbidity rates around the world, as illustrated in "Lek's Story," "The Cries of a Drum," "Mr. Coulibaly's Advice," and "Innocence's Journey." "Amina Ndiaye" and "DOTS" demonstrate the importance of getting treatment and finishing treatment regimens. Illness does not always result from infection, however; "Leilei's Breakfast," "*Azúcar en la sangre*," "Dancing between Cleveland and Standing Rock," and "*Fa'asamoa*" examine the problems the come with chronic illnesses such as diabetes and obesity. "Students Fight Rubella," "The Open Door," and "The Accident" show how sickness and morbidity can be prevented through immunization programs and improved access to health services in underserved areas. "Bathroom Numb," "Little Ashes," and "Envisioning Invisibility" attest to the importance of recognizing less visible behavior-based health problems such as bulimia and smoking. The silent illness—depression, which is one of the most pervasive of our time—is explored throughout the book and in "Overcast Highs" and "Between Cheeseburger and *Burek*" in particular. Finally, "Tuya's Ride" and "The Little *Dhami*" present two excellent examples of how young people can play central roles in improving health in their families and communities.

Although these are a small few of the many health concerns facing our planet, they are certainly global concerns. After reading this book, we hope you have become curious. And we hope that this curiosity is funneled into improving your community in some way. There are many ways to make a difference. A few examples include volunteering, writing letters to your representative, and becoming educated about the many global health problems around the world—in addition to the many solutions (on a small and large scale).

A key component of making a difference begins with understanding the problem. We hope that this book has ignited your interest in exploring global health in a larger capacity. We hope, to quote the epigraph from Paolo Freire at the beginning of this book, that you will learn to "deal critically and creatively with reality and discover how to participate in the transformation of [our] world."

You can learn about additional ways to deal critically with and think creatively about global and local public health problems on our website: www.globalhealthnarratives4change.org or www.ghn4c.org.

Glossary of Selected Words and Concepts

Anorexia nervosa—an eating disorder that leads to a loss of appetite and that is accompanied by fear of being overweight, a disturbed body image, and denial. Anorexia nervosa is most common among individuals between ten to twenty-five years of age.

Buddhism—a religion practiced primarily in South and East Asia that follows the teachings of the Buddha. Buddhists believe that the world is always changing and that one should not try to hold onto things as if they don't change.

Bulimia—episodic binge eating usually followed by behavior designed to negate excessive caloric intake, such as purging via self-induced vomiting or laxative abuse but also sometimes excessive exercising or fasting, which may be followed by feelings of guilt or depression.

Cancer—a class of diseases or disorders characterized by the uncontrolled division of cells that are capable of invading other tissues. Cancer affects people of all ages, but risk increases with age. It is one of the leading causes of death in high-income countries like Japan.

Carbon monoxide (CO)—a colorless, odorless, toxic air pollutant produced by incomplete combustion or burning. Carbon monoxide inhibits the body's ability to absorb oxygen and can cause chest pain and a cough. Inhaling too much carbon monoxide can be lethal.

Cerebral palsy (CP)—refers to a group of disorders that affect a person's ability to move and maintain balance and posture. It is caused by brain damage that occurs during pregnancy or during or shortly after birth and it undermines a child's ability to control her or his muscles. The part of the brain that is damaged determines what parts of the body are affected. The term "cerebral" refers to the brain's two halves, or hemispheres, and "palsy" describes any disorder that impairs control of body movement.

Coma—a state of deep unconsciousness from which a person cannot be awakened that is usually caused by intense illness, injury to a person's head, or abuse of alcohol or drugs. A coma can last from a few hours to several months, and sometimes longer.

Cryptosporidiosis—infection with protozoa. Although this parasite can be spread in several different ways, it is most commonly transmitted through water (drinking and recreational), and *Cryptosporidia* are one of the most frequent causes of waterborne disease. The most common symptoms are prolonged diarrhea, dehydration, fever, and abdominal pain.

Crystal methamphetamine—a colorless, odorless form of d-methamphetamine, a highly addictive synthetic (human-made) stimulant. This drug is abused because of the long-lasting euphoric effects it produces. The drug can cause rapid heart rate, increased blood pressure, and damage to the small blood vessels in the brain—which can lead to stroke.

Dengue fever—a severe disease carried by mosquitoes causing fever, headache, joint pain, and a rash. Dengue fever is the number one killer of children in Southeast Asia.

Depression—a common disorder that presents with depressed mood, loss of interest or pleasure in life, feelings of guilt or low self-worth, disturbed sleep or appetite, low energy, and poor concentration. These problems can become chronic or recurrent and may impair an individual's ability to carry out his or her everyday responsibilities. Depression is among the leading causes of disability worldwide.

Diabetes—a metabolic disorder that is often characterized by "high blood sugar," or glucose. Type 1 (insulin-dependent) diabetics tend to develop the disease early in life and are unable to control blood-sugar levels because their bodies cannot make insulin. Type 1 diabetes is often referred to as juvenile diabetes because of its prevalence in children. Type 2 (noninsulin-dependent) diabetics are older and the disease is often associated with obesity. Insulin is a hormone that converts sugar, starches, and other food into energy needed to keep the body functioning.

Emphysema—a lung disease in which the air sacs are enlarged and damaged. As a result, the body does not get the oxygen it requires. The most common cause is smoking. Treatments, designed to relieve symptoms and prevent complications, include inhalers, oxygen, medications, and sometimes surgery.

Epilepsy—a neurological condition that affects the nervous system, also known as a seizure disorder. People diagnosed with epilepsy have had more than one seizure, and they may have had more than one kind of seizure. A seizure happens when abnormal electrical activity in the brain causes an involuntary change in body movement or function, sensation, awareness, or behavior. Most forms of epilepsy can be treated effectively with medication. In many cultures, epilepsy is a stigmatized disorder affecting entire families.

Ethnicity—a set of characteristics that produces a distinctive culture that a group of people share. In the United States, "ethnicity" generally refers to a subset of the national culture in which people share one or more of the following characteristics: race, nationality, appearance, geography, religion, ancestry, or language. "Ethnicity" sometimes refers to the group of people as well as the culture itself.

Gender-based violence—violence that is directed against a person on the basis of gender or sex. It includes acts that inflict physical, psychological, or sexual harm or suffering, threats of such acts, coercion, and other deprivations of liberty.

Guarani—the name of a group of culturally related indigenous peoples of South America who are distinguished from the related Tupi by their use of the Guarani language. In Paraguay, the Guarani live between the Uruguay River and the Lower Paraguay River.

Guatemalan highlands—western part of Guatemala that includes the large city of Quetzaltenango, also called Xelajú in Mam. This is a mountainous region that is home to many isolated communities with strong indigenous identities.

Hiroshima—the largest city of the largest of Japan's islands, it is most well known throughout the world as the first city in history to be subjected to nuclear warfare, bombed on August 6th, 1945, by a U.S. Air Force B-29 bomber. An estimated eighty thousand people were killed, and 80 percent of the city was heavily damaged. In the months following the bombing, sixty thousand more people died from injuries or radiation poisoning. Today Hiroshima has been rebuilt and is a "peace memorial city."

Human immunodeficiency virus (HIV)—a virus that causes acquired immunodeficiency syndrome, or AIDS. HIV infects and disables the cells of the body's immune system. No medications are currently available to cure HIV or AIDS, but antiretroviral therapies can help people live longer and healthier lives. You cannot get HIV from casual interactions with a person who is HIV positive. Unprotected sex, shared needles, and exposure to contaminated blood increase an individual's risk for infection.

Immune system—the defensive system in a host consisting of nonspecific and specific immune responses. It is composed of widely distributed cells, tissues, and organs that recognize foreign substances and microorganisms and that act to neutralize or destroy them.

Indigenous—cultural groups (and their descendants) who have a historical association with a given region or parts of a region and who formerly inhabited or currently inhabit the region.

Internally displaced person (IDP)—someone who has been forced to leave his or her home because of war or persecution but who has not crossed an international border. If this person crossed a border, he or she would be considered a refugee instead.

Leukemia—a cancer that starts in blood-forming tissue such as the bone marrow and causes large numbers of blood cells to be produced and enter the bloodstream.

Malaria—a parasitic disease transmitted through the bite of infected mosquitoes that often breed in standing water. Symptoms of malaria include fever, chills, and headache. Malaria causes over one million deaths each year. This disease can be fatal, but bed nets, insecticides, and antimalarial drugs are effective tools in fighting and curing malaria in areas where it is transmitted.

Mam—an indigenous group living in the southwestern and western highlands of Guatemala. Many still wear traditional dress and speak Mam.

Mapuche—American Indians of central and southern Chile and southern Argentina known for their lengthy resistance to Spanish colonialism. The name is comprised of two parts, "mapu," which means "land," and "che," which means "people."

Maté—a medicinal and cultural drink of the Indians of South America. The infusion called maté (also often called yerba maté) is prepared by steeping dry leaves (and twigs) of the yerba maté shrub in hot water.

Maternal mortality—the death of a woman while pregnant or within forty-two days of the termination of pregnancy, irrespective of the duration and site of the pregnancy, from any cause related to or aggravated by the pregnancy or its management but not from accidental or incidental causes.

Mercury (Hg)—a naturally occurring element that is found in air, water, and soil. This heavy metal is liquid at normal room temperature and pressure but is so dense that cannon balls float in it. Repeated inhalation of mercury metal vapor affects the human brain, spinal cord, eyes, and kidneys. Swallowing mercury compounds can cause nausea, vomiting, diarrhea, and even severe kidney damage.

Methyl mercury ([CH3Hg]+)— a toxin that has been linked to developmental deficits, such as decreased performance in tests of language skills, decreased memory function, and attention deficits in children exposed in utero. Mercury in the air settles into water or onto land where it can be washed into water. Once deposited, certain microorganisms can change it into methyl mercury, a highly toxic form that accumulates in fish, shellfish, and animals that eat fish. Humans get mercury poisoning by eating contaminated fish.

Midwife—a person who is qualified to supervise, care for, and advise women during pregnancy, labor, and the postpartum period. Midwives undertake preventative measures, examine pregnant women to detect abnormal conditions in mother and child, procure medical assistance, and execute emergency measures in the absence of medical help. They may practice in hospitals, clinics, health units, or in private homes.

Migration (human migration)—the movement of people across a specified boundary for the purpose of establishing a new residence. There are two kinds of migration: international migration (migration between countries) and internal migration (migration within a country).

Nicotine—the drug in tobacco products that produces dependence. Nicotine dependence is the most common form of chemical dependence in the United States. Research suggests that nicotine is as addictive as heroin, cocaine, or alcohol.

Obesity—a disease characterized by above-normal body weight, usually defined as more than 20 percent above what's considered healthy for people of a certain age, height, and bone structure. A person is considered obese if he or she has a body mass index (BMI) of 30 kg/m2 or greater.

Parasite—an organism that lives on or within another organism (the host) and benefits from the association while harming its host. Often the parasite obtains nutrients from the host.

Particulate matter—small particles and droplets in the air that vary in size and shape. Breathing in particulate matter can cause a runny nose, watery eyes, and a hoarse cough. People who already have a cough or who have asthma or bronchitis can end up feeling much worse if they are exposed to particulate matter.

Race—a population of human beings distinguished in some ways from populations of other human beings. People often define themselves in biological, social, and spiritual terms.

Refugee—a person who lives outside his or her country due to persecution associated with race, religion, nationality, membership in a particular social group, or political opinion.

Smoking cessation—giving up smoking tobacco products. A person who quits smoking will greatly reduce his or her risk of developing lung cancer, coronary heart disease, stroke, peripheral vascular disease, and women can reduce their risk for adverse reproductive health outcomes such as infertility or having a low-birth-weight baby.

Structural violence—a form of violence resulting from the systematic ways social institutions prevent individuals, families, and communities from meeting their basic needs. The social domination, political oppression, and economic exploitation that define structural violence result in reduced life spans.

Subsistence farming—a mode of horticulture in which a plot of land is used to produce only enough food for the family working on it. If there is surplus food, it is often sold at local markets or stores.

Trachoma—an infection of the eye caused by the bacterium *Chlamydia trachomatis*. Infection spreads from person to person and is frequently passed from child to child and from child to mother, especially in places where there are shortages of water, numerous flies, and crowded living conditions. The World Heath Organization estimates that approximately 6 million people worldwide have lost their eyesight as a result of trachoma and more than 150 million people are in need of treatment.

Traditional healing—the oldest form of structured medicine—that is, a medicine that has an underlying philosophy and set of principles by which it is practiced. There are many fundamental similarities among traditional healing practices around the world that arise from a profound knowledge of natural laws and an understanding of how these laws influence living things.

Tuberculosis (TB)—an infectious disease that most commonly affects the lungs, caused by the bacterium *Mycobacterium tuberculosis*. TB is spread through the air from one person to another. The bacteria are put into the air when a person with active TB disease of the lungs or throat coughs or sneezes. People nearby may breathe in these bacteria and become infected. Tuberculosis is one of the deadliest and most common infectious diseases today. Many of the people who die from TB are also immunocompromised due to HIV and AIDS.

Typhoid—a bacterial disease of the intestinal track and bloodstream. Typhoid germs are passed in the feces and urine of infected people, and people become infected by drinking water that has become contaminated by sewage. On average seventeen million are affected by typhoid each year.

Urbanization—a population shift from rural to urban environments. In 1950, one-third of the world's people lived in cities. Just fifty years later, this proportion has risen to one-half; by 2050, it is expected that two-thirds of the population, or six billion people, will live in cities.

Waterborne disease—any disease that is spread by the ingestion of water contaminated by human or animal feces or urine containing pathogenic bacteria or viruses; examples include cholera, typhoid, amoebic dysentery, and other diarrheal diseases.

Contributors

Hannah Adams has been drawing small pictures all of her life and studied studio art at Bard College.

Sangogbemi J. Ajamu, MSN candidate, is a U.S. Marine Corps veteran, a priest of the West African indigenous spiritual system Ifa, and a nurse-practitioner student at Vanderbilt University. He plans to serve the underserved and assist in providing quality healthcare to all.

The ArtReach Foundation is an organization devoted to using art therapy to help children who have been traumatized by war, violence, or natural disasters. Its contribution to this volume was the result of work it carried out in Bosnia-Herzegovina from 2000 to 2005 (http://www.artreachfoundation.org).

Lavone G. Bradfield, MPH, MD candidate, studies medicine at the University of North Dakota and plans to practice medicine and public health in an urban health or Indian health facility.

Ryan A. Brown, PhD, is from the Appalachian mountains of Virginia and has studied risk taking, aggression, and substance use among local youths. He is a professor at Northwestern University in the School of Education and Social Policy.

Elizabeth Burpee spent a year and a half working with women and communities in Tijuana, Mexico, through the organization Los Niños International. She currently works as a community organizer in Chicago, Illinois.

Deborah Casanova, MPH, was a Peace Corps volunteer in San Pedro, Paraguay, from 1995 to 1998 and has worked in public health, focusing on HIV/AIDS in South Africa, Rwanda, and Zambia.

Verna Miller Case, PhD, is a professor of animal behavior at Davidson College and takes students to Zambia each summer to learn about public health and medicine at the United Church of Zambia Hospital in Mwandi, Zambia.

Ana Elena Chévez, MD, MPH, worked with the Ministry of Health in El Salvador as the director of the Programa Ampliado de Inmunizaciones (EPI) for eight years and currently works with the World Health Organization on various immunization projects in Guatemala and Nigeria.

Ana Croegaert, PhD, is a cultural anthropologist who examined the social and economic lives of Bosnian refugees in Chicago between 1994 and 2005 and is currently a professor of anthropology at Mount Holyoke.

Matthew Dudgeon, PhD, MPH, MD candidate, spent twenty-eight months examining men and reproductive health in postwar Guatemala in two K'iche' Mayan communities, and he currently studies medicine at the Emory University School of Medicine.

Dorothy Foster, MA, was born and raised in the highlands of Guatemala and has lived and traveled extensively in Africa and Asia with her husband, Dr. Stanley Foster, who worked for the Centers for Disease Control and Prevention. She has dedicated her life to helping people to learn English and adapt to life in the United States.

Leslie Greene, MPH, works with the Center for Global Safe Water at Emory University and conducts public health research and program evaluations to improve water, sanitation, and hygiene-related development programs.

Laurie R. Hibbett, MDiv candidate, studies religion at Duke Divinity School and is interested in Christian ethics, Kierkegaard, and issues related to mental illness, addiction, and eating disorders.

Elizabeth A. Jacobs, MD, MAPP, is a clinician-researcher and assistant professor of medicine at the John H. Stroger Jr. Hospital of Cook County and the Rush University Medical Center where she works with other investigators to design culturally specific research programs and teaches residents and medical students about practicing culturally sensitive medicine.

Dredge Byung'chu Käng, MPH, PhD candidate, studies medical anthropology at Emory University and has worked in HIV prevention, care, and research for over ten years in Thailand and the U.S.; he is interested in issues related to gender, sexuality, social violence, health inequality, and HIV.

Ember Keighley, MPH, MD candidate, is dedicated to helping improve the health and well-being of people in underserved communities globally. She has worked on public health research projects in Samoa, American Samoa, and Mongolia and studies medicine at the University of Michigan.

Brandon Kohrt, MD/PhD candidate, is a technical adviser for the Transcultural Psychosocial Organization (TPO) in Nepal and studies medicine and biocultural anthropology at Emory University. He founded the Atlanta Asylum Network for Torture Survivors, for which he received the Navin Narayan Human Rights Leadership Award from Physicians for Human Rights.

Charlotte Kvasnovsky, MPH/MD candidate, studies medicine and public health at Emory University and is coordinating a study on drug-resistant tuberculosis in South Africa for the Centers for Disease Control's Division of Tuberculosis Elimination. She plans to become a surgeon.

Jie Liu, MPH, works with the Global AIDS Program in China and has worked and conducted research extensively on HIV/AIDS in China.

Kenneth Maes, PhD candidate, studies medical anthropology at Emory University and is conducting research on the motivations of volunteer caregivers of people living with AIDS in Addis Ababa, Ethiopia.

Courtney E. Martin, MA, is the award-winning author of *Perfect Girls, Starving Daughters: The Frightening New Normalcy of Hating Your Body*. She is an adjunct professor of gender studies at Hunter College and was awarded the Elie Wiesel Prize in Ethics in 2002.

Emily Mendenhall, MPH, PhD candidate, has worked on public health research projects in Chile, Zambia, Guatemala, and Chicago. She currently studies medical anthropology at Northwestern University, focusing on health, migration, structural violence, and illness narratives in the Americas.

Maggie Montgomery, PhD, has worked extensively on clean water projects in Tanzania, first under a U.S. Fulbright grant, then through Engineers without Borders as a doctoral student of environmental engineering at Yale University, and now as staff member of the World Health Organization. She believes in clean water and sanitation for all.

Gabriel Okpattah was born in Accra, Ghana, and studies sociology, archaeology, and information studies at the University of Ghana.

Chandra Y. Osborn, PhD, MPH, is a professor at Vanderbilt University Medical School and studies the role of health literacy in racial/ethnic disparities in health care access, disease treatment, and health outcomes. Laufali Virginia Maiava supported her in writing this story.

Amy Patterson, MPH, PhD candidate, was a high school English and biology teacher for four years before beginning a career in public health. She has worked on several projects in Mali, West Africa, and currently studies audience reactions to a series of short fictional films about HIV/AIDS in Africa.

Ajay Pillarisetti, MPH, has worked extensively on environmental health projects in India and Nepal. He is a cofounder of Campus Movie Fest, a nationwide short-film festival for college students. He is currently working on an indoor air quality project in Nepal as a Fulbright scholar.

Jackie Protos, MA, has worked as an English educator with Summerbridge's Students Teaching Students program in Atlanta, Hong Kong, and Boston. She spent a year teaching English in rural Japan and now teaches high school English in Atlanta.

Sarah Raskin, MPH, PhD candidate, has worked extensively on the prevention of violence against women in Tanzania and the United States and currently studies medical anthropology at the University of Arizona. Her areas of interest include violence against women, social services, and public health.

Mary Souder, MA, has worked directly with several individuals suffering with depression and studies counseling psychology at Pacific University. Her work has been strongly influenced by her mother and sister.

Athena Stevens has spent the last few years working with both the Royal Shakespeare Company and the London Underground as lead disability adviser. She has over twenty years of experience in advocating for disability rights and was named Female Athlete of the Year by the United States Cerebral Palsy Athletic Association in 1998.

Alyce Latisha Tucker, MPH, has studied and worked extensively with HIV/AIDS research in Atlanta, Georgia, and currently is working on a national evaluation of a children's mental health services program for a public health consulting firm in Atlanta.

Mary Carleen Veal moved to Bucharest, Romania, in 1993 and has worked with children infected with HIV and with children who have developed AIDS, helping to provide a pioneer home health care program for very poor families. She is a committed pacifist and has been devoted all her life to social justice and human rights.

Nicole Warren, PhD, RN, teaches maternal health in the School of Nursing at Loyola University in Chicago. She is a practicing certified nurse-midwife whose research interests include maternal mortality in Africa and caring for women who have experienced female genital cutting. For more than three years, she lived and worked in Mali, where she gathered stories from midwives based in rural areas.

Kate Winskell, PhD, teaches courses on global health communication, HIV/AIDS, gender, sexuality, and global health at Emory University in Atlanta. With her husband, Daniel Enger, she works for Scenarios from Africa (www.globaldialogues.org), a program that inspires tens of thousands of young Africans to write story lines for short films about the HIV/AIDS epidemic, coordinating communication between the program and African children.

Index